Learning Together
Teaching Pupils with Special Educational Needs in
the Ordinary School

Ann Hodgson
Louise Clunies-Ross
Seamus Hegarty

NFER-NELSON

20 3 342 (371·9)

Published by The NFER-NELSON Publishing Company Ltd.,
Darville House, 2 Oxford Road East,
Windsor, Berkshire SL4 1DF

First published 1984
Reprinted 1985
© *NFER and Schools Council Publications, 1984*
ISBN 0 – 7005 – 0662 – 4
Code 8180 021

Printed in England.

Distributed by Taylor & Francis Inc.,
242 Cherry Street, Philadelphia, PA 19106-1906.
Tel: (215) 238 0939. Telex: 244489.

CONTENTS

v

Acknowledgements

The team would like to thank all those who have helped in any way with this report.In particular we wish to thank Schools Council and NFER Board of Management for jointly providing funds for the project. Thanks are also due to the LEAs and schools who gave us access and for their help in providing information and opportunity to examine their practice.

Some mention must be made of the members of the advisory committee, listed below, for their very helpful suggestions and advice throughout the project and on the valuable comments addressed to the preliminary drafts of the manuscript.

Helen Carter	Chairperson, Schools Council
Jim Conway	Adviser, Barnsley
Alan Collinge-Hill	Senior Master, Holmer Green Secondary
John Moore	Senior Lecturer, Oxford Polytechnic
John Fish	HMI
Chris Marshall	HMI
Colin Smith	Dept. of Education, Birmingham

Similarly, our thanks to the readers of the final manuscript, Di Moses, NFER and Peter Davies, Sheffield for their very valuable and detailed comments.

Finally, our thanks to the secretarial staff who so efficiently handled all clerical matters concerning the project and for all the hard work involved in preparing the manuscript.

Foreword

The traditional dichotomy between special education and mainstream education has been challenged by the Education Act 1981, which came into force on April 1st 1983, and its accompanying circular and regulations. Radical changes in the British educational system are not achieved overnight but the framework provided by this legislation marks a major development in special education thinking and practice. If what is enacted is also implemented far-reaching changes will be wrought.

An initial concern of the Act is with terminology. It speaks of children having special educational needs rather than being handicapped. This is more than a semantic change because the traditional categories of handicap (educationally subnormal, blind, physically handicapped and so on) have limited educational relevance. A child is deemed to have special educational needs if he or she 'has a learning difficulty which calls for special educational provision to be made'. Children having a learning difficulty are defined as those who have significantly greater difficulty in learning than the majority of children of their age, or who have a disability which hinders them in using the educational facilities available to age peers. Special education provision is defined as 'provision which is additional to, or otherwise different from, the educational provision made generally' for age peers in the locality.

The Act requires LEAs to identify children with special educational needs and to arrange for appropriate special educational provision. Procedures are laid down for assessing the child's educational needs. Where an assessment has been carried out and special educational provision deemed necessary, the authority must make a formal Statement of the child's educational needs and how they are to be met. Statements are to be reviewed at least annually.

One of the most significant requirements of the Act relates to integration. LEAs have a duty to make special education provision for all those requiring it in ordinary schools, so long as certain conditions are met. School authorities in turn have a duty to secure that pupils with special educational needs engage in the activities of the school together with other pupils.

All this calls for major changes within schools and throughout the educational system. This book focuses on the response that schools must make, particularly with regard to curriculum modification. By documenting and analysing practice in those schools that are already well under way it may serve to guide and stimulate those who have still some distance to travel.

Chapter 1
Background to the Study

> Pupils with special needs do not need integration.
> They need education.
>
> (Hegarty *et al.*, 1981)

Beyond integration

The principle of integration has made great strides in recent
years. From being a rallying cry for those with a vision of change
in special education, it has become the new orthodoxy. It is
special schools that have to justify their existence now, not
integration initiatives. The prevailing assumption, enshrined in
legislation, is that all pupils should be considered first for
placement in an ordinary school, and only when that is
problematic or appears likely to be so should a special school
placement be made. Inevitably, there is a gap between theory
and practice, and many pupils still go to special schools who
need not. But what of those pupils with special needs who go to
ordinary schools? For them the principle of integration *has* been
invoked, and they would seem to be the clear beneficiaries of
educational reform.

A fundamental distinction has to be made between integration
as placement and integration as education. Attention has
understandably been focused on the former. Given two parallel
and separate education systems – mainstream and special – it is
necessary first to desegregate children and to ensure that they
have the opportunity for normal socialisation. This can be
achieved in some measure by changing the *place* of formal
education. 'Locational' integration does eliminate some barriers
of distance and separation and marks a necessary first step in
desegregating pupils with special needs.

This is no more than a first step, however. Integration is
essentially about schooling. Pupils with special needs, just like

other pupils, go to school in order to be taught and to learn. The task of schools is to promote pupils' learning and to create the conditions under which appropriate learning takes place – for all pupils. If a school is not achieving this it is failing in its primary role, regardless of whatever else it may be doing.

These considerations take on particular force when one looks at the history of special education and the institutional segregation which has figured so prominently in it. Initially, segregated provision was set up for children with severe handicaps, usually sensory in origin. This marked a considerable advance at the time since the alternative was no schooling whatsoever. As universal education spread and schools were faced with a wider range of pupil learning and behaviour, the limitations of the mainstream school system became apparent. Very many schools were neither equipped nor willing to educate all pupils who came their way. Accordingly, many pupils were excluded from mainstream schools. In order to cater for them and to provide the school placements to which they were entitled in law, the special school sector had to expand. Given the mainstream rejection of pupils arriving in this way, it was to be expected that these schools would be set apart from the mainstream and would develop in a segregated way.

There were other reasons for this segregation from the mainstream. The prevailing understanding of handicap was in terms of *defect*. Physical and sensory impairments were seen as imposing specific limits on cognitive development, while learning difficulties were conceived in terms of mental deficiency. A handicap was an enduring characteristic and indeed one of the most significant facts about a person. Handicapped children were different in kind from other children, so it made sense to develop a separate educational system for them. Running alongside these ideological considerations and helping to underpin them was the claimed administrative convenience of grouping children with similar handicaps and concentrating in one place the special resources they needed.

Whatever the reasons for segregation and regardless of how well special schools fitted the prevailing requirements, the overriding consideration in any move toward integration is that ordinary schools were inadequate in the first instance. If pupils were removed from ordinary schools because their needs could not be met there, it makes little sense to return them without close examination of what the ordinary school has to offer and if necessary making changes. Put more directly, what this means is that integration requires educational reform. Ordinary schools have to 'stretch' themselves, to become more comprehensive, so that they are able to cope with a wider range of educational needs than before and to ensure that pupils with special needs gain the benefits of being in a mainstream environment.

It is unfortunate that the most obvious manifestations of integration programmes are sometimes the overt physical ones – ramps, hearing aid technology, special pieces of equipment. No matter how essential these may be, they are secondary if not peripheral to the educational task. A youngster may need ramps to get round a school independently and specialized equipment to record work in the classroom, but these are administrative rather than educational concerns. What matters essentially is the quality of education on offer and how well it relates to individual pupil needs. So the most important developments have to occur at the level of curriculum – what pupils are taught and why, how they are to be taught and how their progress is monitored.

This curriculum development must be carried out afresh by and in ordinary schools. Some special schools have built up sophisticated curricular provision, within a segregated context, for pupils with special needs, and this can be a significant resource for ordinary schools to draw on. It must be no more than a resource, however, and not a blueprint. Meeting special educational needs in an ordinary school is a different enterprise from meeting them in a special school and operates with different opportunities and constraints. Success must be seen in terms of capitalizing on these opportunities and circumventing the constraints, not in reproducing the educational environment of the special school.

If pupils with special needs attending ordinary schools are to have access to the mainstream curriculum *and* receive an education appropriate to their needs, staff must be able to develop appropriate programmes of work and possess the teaching skills to cater for a wide range of aptitudes and needs. They have to decide what each pupil should learn, select appropriate teaching strategies and learning resources, and monitor subsequent progress. Some schools will have specialist teachers in post to guide and support their colleagues in these demanding tasks. Many will not, however, the more so as integration becomes more common and increasing numbers of pupils with special educational needs attend their neighbourhood schools. The result is that many more class teachers may find themselves in the position of having to teach individual pupils with special needs without having adequate recourse to specialist in-house support.

Research

Despite the volume of research on the topic of integration, there has been little that is directed centrally at this enterprise. The bulk of the research has been either comparative or descriptive. (For a recent overview, cf. Hegarty and Pocklington, 1981.) American research in particular has focused on efficacy studies, asking the apparently simple question: Is a pupil with a given handicapping condition better educated in a mainstream setting alongside age peers or in a segregated setting alongside 'handicap peers'? Aside from the methodological limitations of such studies and the inconclusiveness of their findings taken overall, their contribution to curriculum development and practical work in the classroom has been limited. Typically, they have taken two groups of pupils, one in a mainstream setting and a matched group in a segregated setting, and compared them in terms of specific aspects of academic achievement or social development. Such studies could inform the teaching process if specific teaching variables were the subject of comparison. When comparison is made, however, in an undifferentiated way on the basis of the total setting, there is little of practical relevance for the classroom teacher.

Descriptive studies carry more promise of relevance, at least when they move beyond quantitative reporting. Traditionally, descriptive studies have focused on *populations* of children and gathered information of prime interest to planners and policy makers. There is a growing interest, however, in the study of *provision*. This is exemplified by those case studies of integration programmes which combine description, analysis and recommendations for action. Recent examples include Jamieson *et al.*, 1977, Kiernan and Kavanagh, 1977, Hegarty, Pocklington and

Lucas, 1982 and Pocklington and Hegarty, 1983. While such studies mark a step toward the practitioner their usefulness for the class teacher is still limited. The focus tends to be on organizational and structural features, on setting up and resourcing programmes and on the extent to which pupils are actually integrating.

The present study

The need, then, is for research that focuses on the tasks faced by class teachers as a result of increased integration. The initial context was provided by Programme Four within the Schools Council's curriculum development work over the period 1980–83. This programme, entitled Individual Pupils, comprised various projects 'united by a concern for individuals who, for some reason, make exceptional demands on their teachers' skill'. The programme encompassed gifted pupils, pupils from ethnic minorities and disruptive pupils, but a major focus was on pupils with special educational needs in the sense of learning difficulties and handicapping conditions that affect learning. A particular concern with regard to the education of such pupils was to assist teachers in the task of making appropriate modifications to the curriculum in mainstream settings.

Following discussions with NFER staff, a project was devised which was funded jointly by the two organizations. The project brief was

i) to examine teaching strategies that are relevant to managing the learning of pupils with a wide variety of needs
ii) to clarify the process by which the curriculum of the ordinary school is modified to take account of these pupils' needs
iii) to produce a report that will detail the practical and theoretical aspects of this extension of the ordinary teacher's role.

The research was carried out by research officers at NFER and ran for a period of two years from January 1982.

For the purposes of the study the term 'pupil with special needs' was not defined tightly. This was a deliberate tactic. The terminology of the Education Act 1981 was gaining currency but it was – and still is – far from universal. The aim in any case was to study modifications to the curriculum for those pupils for whom schools themselves judged that additional learning support was necessary. Schools defined this group in different ways. In some cases they were encountering such pupils for the first time and were literally trying to 'integrate' them; in other cases such pupils had been at the school for many years and were an integral part of it. While many of the group would fall within the two per cent or so of pupils conventionally deemed to have pronounced difficulties, this was certainly not true of all. In terms of the established descriptions of special needs the group encompassed pupils with learning difficulties, both moderate and specific, pupils with physical handicaps and pupils with hearing and visual impairments. A general characterization of the group would be that it encompassed pupils with complex learning difficulties who required extra support in their learning.

The study was conducted in two major phases. First, information was gathered about pupils with special needs who were already being educated in ordinary schools. Sources included findings from other recent research projects, contacts which had been made while engaged in them and published information. In addition, information was sought from a number of LEAs concerning the nature and extent of integration within their schools. In these ways and with the help and recommendations of advisers, advisory teachers and education officers, a substantial number of ordinary schools were identified in which pupils with special educational needs were enrolled.

During the initial phase the team visited 76 schools in 21 LEAs in England and Wales in order to explore with headteachers and their staffs school policy on educating pupils with special needs and its practice in the light of prevailing conditions. We also took the opportunity to look round the school and to see some of the pupils at work and at play, noting any particular difficulties presented by the physical environment of the school and observing also the adaptations, alterations and additions which had in some cases been undertaken in order to make provision for pupils with special needs. Details such as ramps for wheelchairs, handrails on stairways to aid the visually impaired, the location of a resources area, the position of a teaching room for the hearing impaired were all best understood by observation.

It was obviously an impossible task to make individual studies of over 70 schools and so the initial sample was reduced to 26 for the second phase of the study. The schools chosen for this phase were not intended to be a nationally representative sample. Some of the practice selected for study was relatively unusual but was purposely chosen so as to broaden the range of possibilities under consideration. It is only in this specific sense that the sample was intended to be representative. Moreover, the sample was confined to situations where pupils were spending at least some part of the day being taught alongside age peers in a mainstream setting. We were not concerned with those forms of integration where pupils were enrolled in a school but taught entirely separately within it in a special class or unit.

We also felt it to be particularly important to use schools which had on roll pupils whose degree of handicap affected their education or which had a number of pupils with a variety of special needs. Some mainstream schools chosen had established links with local special schools and offered additional interest in this respect. Additionally we maintained a balance between primary and secondary sector schools and included those with separate units for pupils with special needs where pupils spent considerable time in mainstream as well as those in which all pupils were based in mainstream classes.

During the in-depth case studies considerable time was spent in observing pupils with special needs at work in ordinary classes, receiving back-up support and also receiving specialist teaching. We noted any special resources in use and, in discussion with teachers, documented the strategies they found effective, the resources they found particularly useful and the kinds of back-up support and information they were able to draw upon.

The recording procedure adopted was similar in all schools in so far as visits were made for a number of days in order that a pupil – or pupils – with special needs could be observed in lessons which included the basic skills of language and number and practical work as in art, craft or home economics and, where appropriate, in science and humanities lessons. In this way major curricular areas were covered and pupils were monitored in a variety of circumstances in which they were called upon to exercise different skills, to employ different kinds of problem solving techniques and to use a variety of resources for learning. A pupil's response to a given task was noted, not only in terms of perceived academic progress but also in the exercise of communication skills, motor skills and social skills.

Extensive discussions were held with the teachers in charge of pupils with special needs, where such existed, and with mainstream staff. Discussions encompassed teachers' aims and specific objectives for these pupils, teaching strategies found to be helpful and details of any problems encountered. Where teaching problems had been met and subsequently overcome, information was elicited on the strategies and systems adopted. Where possible, these discussions took place straight after periods of classroom observation. Visits were made to certain schools over a period of four terms, during which time the progress of individual pupils was monitored and the growth and development of specific provision for pupils with special needs recorded. A series of visits also gave time for discussions with ancillaries and staff from external agencies. The final months of the project were devoted to writing up the results, making final visits to a number of schools and holding a series of conferences at which selected findings were presented to LEA officers and advisers and to teachers.

Part One
Academic Organization

Chapter 2
Pupil Grouping

The groups in which pupils spend their school day provide educational settings in which learning takes place, socialization occurs and friendships are forged. School policy on the most appropriate structure for teaching, recreation and pastoral groups can and does vary widely, reflecting a school's aims for its pupils as well as its ability to achieve these within the constraints of staffing level, timetable and teaching space.

The way in which pupils were grouped for teaching purposes was an initial focus of inquiry in the schools under study. Pupils with special needs who joined their age peers in mainstream classes were taught in groups which differed considerably in size and in composition. Mixed ability classes were most commonly found in primary schools and in the first three years of secondary schools; bands, each containing a more restricted range of ability, were chiefly adopted in middle and secondary schools while sets, structured according to pupils' different abilities in specific subjects, were most usually found in secondary schools. Option groups, based upon pupils' subject choices and most common in secondary schools, sometimes contained a wide range of ability but more usually comprised pupils from part of the ability range. In only a few cases were secondary school pupils streamed on a measure of general ability for all academic subjects.

It was common for both primary and secondary schools to organize different kinds of teaching groups for different areas of the curriculum, while pastoral groups were frequently structured on separate criteria again, so that pupils were members of several different groups. The group in which a pupil registered was not necessarily that in which he or she spent most of the day. For example, some pupils registered in 'special needs' groups based in a unit and then spent part of each day in mainstream classes. In some schools registration groups were vertically structured, creating a 'family' atmosphere and a caring environment which head teachers considered to be particularly helpful for pupils with special needs. In other schools pupils registered in the mixed ability groups in which they were subsequently taught for most of each day but within which they were often regrouped for different areas of the curriculum.

Some kinds of teaching groups were perceived by staff to provide particularly suitable educational settings for pupils with special needs. In mixed ability classes, for example, teachers were accustomed to planning for a group whose individual responses to the curriculum were very different; they were used to varying their teaching strategies to accommodate pupils' individual needs and in this situation a pupil with special educational needs did not constitute a unique problem – merely another kind of individual need. Work was often based on individual assignments, so that the element of competition was absent and pupils were not pressured to keep up with classmates. Group work provided opportunities for pupils to learn how to cooperate and were a particular feature of primary schools in which mixed ability teaching was a major feature. In periods of class discussion, teachers were accustomed to accept a wide range of responses from pupils, so all were encouraged to participate. Team teaching was an organizational feature of some schools, with the result that pupils could be regrouped on specific criteria for activities in different areas of the curriculum. In addition, pupils in a team teaching situation were able to meet staff other than their class teacher and become used to working with pupils from other classes.

Several head teachers considered that mixed ability classes made easier the task of allocating pupils with special needs to mainstream groups. The widest possible choice of classes was available and criteria other than academic achievement could be taken into consideration. Teachers' personalities and attitude toward special needs, class size, the nature of the curriculum and the number of other pupils with special needs in the class were commonly taken into account when deciding on a placement for individual pupils. In banded classes, where a more restricted range of ability was represented, teachers commonly adopted similar pedagogical practices to those outlined above; pupils were viewed as individuals and in general this was considered to be an appropriate educational setting for pupils with special needs.

Subject-specific sets, which were often smaller than the average size of class organized in the school as a whole, were seen to provide an opportunity for teachers to allocate a pupil to a teaching group appropriate to his or her level of academic attainment in a given subject. Smaller groups offered obvious advantages in that more individual attention could be given to a pupil, while from a practical point of view a classroom with a smaller group of pupils allowed greater possibility for furniture to be rearranged to accommodate the needs of a pupil with physical handicap or sensory deficit which necessitated the use of special and often bulky resources and equipment. In addition, pupils could join sets in some subjects and receive alternative specialist teaching in others as deemed necessary. Sets offered a valuable flexibility in this respect, with teachers able to match pupils and sets on an individual basis.

Streamed classes were rarely encountered in our study and were generally regarded as providing a less flexible environment for pupils with special needs than the other forms of grouping outlined above.

Besides the composition of a class, teachers and head teachers identified certain features which favoured the process of integration. It was helpful if there were not more than two pupils with special needs allocated to any one class; more than two pupils resulted in greater demands on teacher time than could be accommodated without possible detriment to other pupils in the class. It was widely acknowledged that two pupils with similar special needs could be accommodated more easily than two pupils whose individual educational needs were very different. For example, with two hearing impaired pupils in a group, a teacher could concentrate on increasing the visual content of a lesson in order to facilitate their participation; but if one of the pupils was deaf and the other visually impaired, part of the value of this tactic would be lost, and the teacher would require an additional focus on auditory input. While the use of a range of teaching techniques and of resources is generally accepted as good teaching practice, the presence of pupils with very different special needs in one group places heavy demands upon a teacher. Frequently these demands cannot be met adequately without additional assistance.

There were other reasons for limiting the numbers of pupils with special needs allocated to each mainstream class. Both heads and teachers were aware of the potential fire hazards presented by wheelchairs, and for this reason preferred to have only one pupil who used a wheelchair in each class. Similarly, other pupils with limited mobility were considered to be better placed among several different groups rather than attending the same mainstream class where they would undoubtedly place an additional responsibility on the teacher in terms of oversight for their safety. In workshops and craft rooms, there was often insufficient space to manoeuvre more than one wheelchair or to accommodate more than one welfare assistant. Some practical subjects were perceived to pose problems of safety for certain pupils and here again it was considered necessary to restrict the number of such pupils in a given group. Teachers in practical science laboratories and in craft workshops were especially aware of their added responsibilities with regard to the personal safety of pupils with special needs, especially those with sensory deficit, limited motor control and restricted mobility.

Head teachers indicated that they attempted to place a pupil with a form or class teacher who was sympathetic to their needs and preferably whose personality was such that the pupil was likely to settle in quickly and relate well to the teacher. They also considered the composition of the class as a whole, as regards attitude and ethos as well as academic standard.

An important factor in this context was the personality of the integrating pupil. Teachers who had monitored the integration of pupils on an individual basis emphasized the vital part that this played in the success with which a pupil integrated. A pupil with an outgoing and cheerful personality invariably settled into mainstream groups and gained acceptance more readily than a pupil who was withdrawn and shy. It was also perceived as helpful to let a pupil join mainstream groups gradually, perhaps on a subject-by-subject basis, providing encouragement and support and monitoring progress by observation, by consultation with the mainstream teacher and by discussion with the pupil. In those schools where pupils with special needs had been present for a number of years, it was policy to place pupils first into those curricular areas which gave opportunity for creative activities and for cooperative team or group work, and in which there was a chance for social skills to be developed. Art, crafts, PE and games were typically those areas of the curriculum for which pupils first joined mainstream peers. Subsequently, pupils were introduced to other curricular areas, depending upon their reactions to and progress in a mainstream setting.

Thus, the nature of the subject, the personalities of the pupil and of the receiving teacher, together with the ethos of the group which a pupil joined and the nature of the special needs presented by that pupil, were all factors which were taken into account in developing individual pupils' programmes of work. For some pupils, especially those of secondary age, it was additionally considered important to establish that they could 'hold their own' academically in the mainstream group in which they were placed. Staff explained that pupils' confidence was boosted by the knowledge that they could succeed in their academic work in mainstream classes; this enhanced their self-image and encouraged them to contribute to class work and so to participate in all aspects of mainstream classroom life.

It is difficult to conceive of an ideal way of grouping pupils and organizing their learning which will meet the requirements of all who have special educational needs. Much depends upon school size, the number of pupils on roll with special needs, the nature and variety of those needs and the problems they present in educational terms. In addition, a school's staffing establishment, curriculum and timetable, together with the physical layout of the school site, all have a bearing on what it is possible to achieve.

The diversity of organizational patterns can be described in terms of a loose continuum from mainstream to segregated provision. Eight patterns can be distinguished on the basis of the provision observed.

  i) Mainstream placement with any extra educational support for individual pupils provided by means of an improved pupil/teacher ratio.

ii) Mainstream placement with pupil support for specific curricular areas. Care support as necessary. Teacher appointed with specific responsibility for pupils with special educational needs.

iii) Mainstream placement and withdrawal for specialist teaching to a resource area or to peripatetic staff. Care support as necessary.

iv) Mainstream base, attending special unit part-time for 'on site' specialist teaching. Care support as necessary.

v) Unit/special class base and mainstream classes part-time. Care support as necessary.

vi) Unit/special class base throughout. Care support as necessary.

vii) Mainstream school as base and special school part-time.

viii) Special school as base and mainstream school part-time.

These patterns are not totally separate from each other. They overlap in practice, and provision in a given school can comprise elements of several different patterns. Caution should be exercised too in viewing the listing as a continuum. Depending on what facet of the provision is in focus – amount of individual teaching support, time spent with peers, departure from mainstream school organization – it could be placed at different points along the continuum. For example, a pupil who is based in the mainstream might spend the greater part of the day withdrawn for specialist teaching, while another who is based in a unit could well be attending a majority of mainstream lessons. What the listing does provide is a convenient way of categorizing the diversity of organizational arrangements that schools make to accommodate pupils with special needs. This in turn facilitates the exploration of the implications of different forms of provision for both pupil and teacher.

i) *Mainstream placement with any extra educational support for individual pupils provided by means of an improved pupil/teacher ratio.*

In these situations schools were observed to cope in three ways.

a) Where pupils were enrolled whose special needs were minor – arising for example from mild physical or sensory impairment – schools chose to use additional staff time in a way that would help all teachers and all pupils. A common practice was to timetable the additional staff member so that smaller class groups could be taught in a particular subject. Basic skills was the most usual area of the curriculum to benefit in this way.

b) In a number of schools the staff member was used to give support in mainstream to *any* pupil who required help. Where pupils' needs were minor and individual help was likely to be required infrequently, using extra teaching time in a flexible way as part of the mainstream teaching establishment was a helpful means of providing support to all pupils.

c) In a few schools the extra staffing allocation was attached to an existing remedial department where special help was already available for pupils with learning difficulties or for whom English was a second language. In this situation the additional staffing could readily be used where it was most needed, either as additional help for pupils with literacy or language problems or as extra support for individual pupils as and when required.

Attaching the additional staff members to an existing department was perceived to have several advantages. These teachers became part of the school, and they had a base from which to work as well as ready contact with other staff. In addition, where the teachers worked part-time only it was particularly helpful that they were attached to a faculty or department. As the number of pupils with special needs is likely to fluctuate over time, a member of a department can share knowledge and expertise with other staff as time allows, and when not required to assist pupils with specific needs can develop his or her own skills in new directions.

ii) *Mainstream placement with pupil support for specific curricular areas. Care support as necessary. Teacher appointed with specific responsibility for pupils with special educational needs.*

In schools where there were a number of pupils with special

educational needs it was not uncommon for a teacher who did
not necessarily teach the pupils or run a special department to be
appointed with responsibility for oversight of their education.
This arrangement allowed considerable flexibility, since the
designated teacher could provide in-class support either in
person or by allocating ancillary or welfare help, could offer
advice on teaching approaches and acquire resource materials
and specialist equipment. This teacher necessarily held a wide
brief as the needs of pupils were often very disparate and their
individual support requirements differed widely. However, the
emphasis in all schools with this kind of arrangement was that
both pupils and teachers should be part of the whole school.
Pupils registered in the mainstream and were taught throughout
by mainstream staff, while the specialist teacher correspondingly
taught mainstream classes and confined him/herself to an
advisory role with regard to pupils with special needs. In this way
the teacher acted very much as a reference point rather than as a
direct teaching support.

In a few schools responsibility for pupils with special needs
was shared with some other role. For example, one designated
teacher was deputy head, another was already in charge of the
school's remedial department and a third organized remedial
maths teaching. An inherent danger in this kind of dual role,
particularly where the member of staff is established as the
remedial specialist in the school, is that teachers can associate the
pupil who has special needs with the remedial department. The
role requirements of such a teacher are wider than those which
have traditionally constituted the work of teachers in charge of
remedial departments, and include considerable liaison with
ordinary teachers in school and with service agencies beyond it
as well as inservice work with colleagues.

iii)   *Mainstream placement and withdrawal for specialist teaching to a
resource area or to peripatetic staff. Care support as necessary.*

Under this arrangement a pupil with special needs is withdrawn
from the mainstream for periods of specialist teaching, either by
a member of school staff or by a peripatetic teacher. The major
difference between this arrangement and the ones previously

outlined is in the location of the resources being utilized. Instead of bringing resources and expertise into the mainstream, pupils move away from their peers for a time in order to receive help elsewhere. The research indicated that this arrangement had evolved in preference to others in the following situations:

a) where the school had no designated teacher on the staff and no source of professional expertise other than the peripatetic teaching service to call upon and

b) where there were a number of pupils on roll who had similar special education needs.

There were, in addition, a number of schools where provision for special needs was made almost entirely by means of peripatetic teaching input. In some schools, of course, peripatetic staff visited in order to supplement school-based learning programmes already established, to arrange for the provision of specialist equipment to individual pupils and to advise on teaching strategies. Their expertise was valued but many staff believed that it was not fully utilized since there was so little opportunity for discussion with them.

iv) *Mainstream base, attending special unit part-time for 'on-site' specialist teaching. Care support as necessary.*

This type of provision for pupils with special educational needs, together with type v) which follows, is very widespread. Pupils all register in mainstream groups and attend a special unit to receive teaching in specific areas of the curriculum as required. There is a flexibility in this arrangement in so far as pupils can receive specialist teaching in individual subjects according to their need. They can join their peers for a greater or lesser part of their timetable, and there is opportunity to alter the balance as pupils' needs change. Specialist units were supervised and run by a teacher appointed with responsibility for pupils with special needs. Care support was usually available in the form of welfare assistants and in many schools ancillary help in the classroom was also provided. Such units may be physically located in purpose-built or converted classrooms, sited centrally or on the periphery of the school buildings. It was not their situation, however, which distinguished them from other forms of special provision, but their academic and administrative structure. Units provided a specialist teaching and care facility which was wider than that given to pupils within a faculty or subject department. Especially for hearing impaired pupils, a special unit could act as a back-up resource rather than a base, with specialist staff keeping in touch with mainstream teacher and the pupils themselves in order to ascertain any specific teaching or learning problems. We found that it was common for hearing impaired pupils at secondary level to attend a unit for English and also during mainstream foreign language lessons, when they received language or vocabulary work or were given back-up support in specific subjects. In primary schools, specialist teachers focused on speech and language development and use was also made of peripatetic speech therapists. This kind of system would appear to be particularly suitable for providing support for pupils with sensory impairments, as it enabled tuition in specific skills to be provided on an individual basis tailored to a pupil's changing needs. In many cases, especially at secondary level, timetabling was straightforward as back-up teaching could be provided during mainstream foreign language lessons.

v)   *Unit/special class base and mainstream classes part-time. Care support as necessary.*

While the timetabled outcome of this type of provision for a pupil may look very similar to that discussed in iv) above, there are important differences of attitude and emphasis. A pupil who registers in a special unit uses this as a base in contrast with other pupils who are part of a class or tutor group. In the eyes of age peers and mainstream staff the pupil is indeed 'special' and to a degree different by virtue of the fact that his form tutor is a 'special teacher' and his immediate peer group a specially selected one. However, units such as this were by no means always isolated or separate from the mainstream, and teacher cooperation was a well-developed feature of some examples of this provision. Units were generally small, with pupils following individual programmes. Back-up support in the mainstream for those integrating on an individual basis was commonly available, given by ancillary helpers or by specialist staff.

vi)   *Unit/special class base throughout. Care support as necessary.*

In the course of the research a number of schools were encountered where there was no classroom integration but there were opportunities for pupils with special needs to socialize with mainstream peers. This form of provision was most common where pupils had moderate learning difficulties or communication problems or where they presented behavioural problems. Thus, one secondary school made provision for pupils with learning difficulties within a special slow learner department and provided the additional facility of a short-stay sanctuary for those who exhibited behavioural problems. Both of these departments liaised chiefly with the pastoral system, and links with mainstream staff were minimal. Since the focus of this research is on integration, only brief mention is necessary here.

vii)   *Mainstream school as base and special school part-time.*

These initiatives were new, and at the time of our research teachers in both special and mainstream schools were still exploring the most useful ways of cooperating over the education of individual pupils with special needs. In the examples studied the schools involved were all located within a few minutes' walk of each other, so that pupils were able to travel easily between buildings. The schemes had grown from the realisation that staff expertise in special schools could do much to meet the learning needs of some pupils in mainstream schools and that the opportunities for small group or individual tuition which were available in special schools constituted a valuable additional resource which could be tapped by mainstream schools.

viii)   *Special school as base and mainstream school part-time.*

This likewise is a relatively novel form of provision. Initiatives of this kind are growing in number, however, and our research would suggest that this is potentially a fruitful area and one where a sharing of expertise can enrich the educational experience of not only the pupil with special needs but all pupils in the mainstream. Staff in both sectors reported that they found their new roles both interesting and stimulating. As a general principle, experience has shown that integration was more successful where two pupils joined a class together, as they gave each other moral support especially on those occasions when the special school teacher was not present. Again, the schools in the examples studied were quite close to each other. Staff in both sectors emphasized the importance of liaison and adequate preparation beforehand. While the new roles of staff in this and the preceding model were still being explored and established, it is clear that links between mainstream and special schools could be developed further for the benefit of pupils with special needs.

Chapter 3
Organization of Supplementary Teaching

A number of schools judged it necessary to make arrangements for supplementary teaching outside mainstream lessons. This took different forms depending upon the pupil's age, level of development and the specific nature of the handicapping condition. While in general staff sought to provide the requisite support within the classroom, withdrawing the pupil as little as possible, there were occasions when it was felt that there was much to be gained by giving the pupil extra help, usually on an individual basis, outside the classroom. This support was provided by specialist teachers, by ancillary helpers and, less usually, by subject staff.

The main aim of back-up teaching was to provide pupils with a level of competence in basic skills and to equip them with the requisite subject-specific information so that they could take a full part in mainstream lessons. Support teaching outside the mainstream classroom was considered necessary for a variety of reasons. For example, pupils with sensory impairment do not receive the same level of visual or auditory stimulus as their sighted and hearing peers and can experience a delay in cognitive development which is apparent in their limited breadth of vocabulary and in their restricted level of conceptual understanding. In addition the motor skills of visually impaired pupils are often slow to develop and some pupils with impaired hearing may require considerable practice in speech production if they are to be encouraged to participate in mainstream lessons. Pupils with learning difficulties can experience problems in understanding the tasks set, and additional help in developing listening, reading and comprehension skills can be of great benefit. Pupils with physical handicaps, as well as receiving in-class support, frequently need more time than their peers to complete assignments in addition to the use of special equipment such as electric typewriters.

The type of support given varied, as did the length of time for which a pupil received it. Some pupils were timetabled to spend a specific number of lessons each week receiving this kind of support, while others had need of extra or alternative tuition far less often. For some pupils, a need for additional help arose largely as a result of the use of a particular kind of resource or teaching mode, while for others more regular help was needed to enable them to sustain progress in the mainstream.

In organizational terms, support given outside the classroom has implications for both staff and pupils as well as for those concerned with timetable arrangements and staffing allocations. It requires close cooperation between the support teacher and subject staff vis-à-vis the aims and content of the planned mainstream lessons. Also, the subject teacher has to adjust to the fact that additional support is required for some pupils for part of the time, and the pupils themselves must be willing to leave the mainstream in order to receive it. For such support schemes to operate smoothly and satisfactorily the timetable should be sufficiently flexible to accommodate pupils' needs for alternative teaching and to permit the release of staff to provide this facility. Teaching space is necessary, and rooms which can be used by visiting peripatetic staff and by support teachers within the school must be so designated.

This supplementary teaching was organized in four main ways: pre-lesson teaching; supplementary teaching provided during a mainstream lesson; post-lesson teaching; pre-lesson and post-lesson support.

Pre-lesson teaching

Preparation of a pupil by the provision of extra teaching prior to a mainstream lesson usually took the form of individual tuition and was most commonly employed for pupils with sensory impairment and those with learning difficulties. In order to provide the most appropriate tuition for each pupil, support staff needed to know what was planned for the mainstream lesson(s), and it was therefore very important to facilitate liaison between support and subject staff in order that two kinds of information might be exchanged. First, support staff required advance knowledge of the content to be covered together with copies of resource materials where appropriate, so that vocabulary and concepts could be checked through with the pupil. Secondly, class teachers needed to know what the chief problem areas were likely to be for a given pupil or pupils and to become acquainted with the kind of specialist preparation that was planned. A timetabled meeting for this exchange of information was rarely possible; staff generally liaised informally regarding individual pupils' preparation and progress. Meetings at lunchtime and after school were organized in some schools.

Pre-lesson teaching was built in to the timetables of pupils and teacher in various ways. For example, where hearing impaired pupils spent one or more periods per day in a specialist unit, the teacher in charge requested details of each half term's work plan from those subject staff who taught the pupils, together with copies of the relevant texts. Working through these herself, she listed new and potentially difficult words and concepts, introducing these individually to pupils before they were first presented to the whole mainstream group. It was found that this strategy did much to increase pupils' confidence and participation in mainstream lessons. However, it was recognized that the scheme was expensive in terms of teacher time and that it made extra demands on mainstream staff in terms of assembling resources and providing the specialist teacher with details of the planned work. Considerable demands were also made on the specialist teacher who had to learn about a range of different subject areas so that she could analyse the projected topics and extract key concepts and vocabulary.

One secondary school, in which pupils with learning difficulties and some who had additional emotional problems were enrolled, adopted this strategy to encourage the full participation of these pupils in mainstream lessons. Pupils were taught first in a group smaller than the mainstream one, with the focus on 'the mechanics of interpersonal relationships'. Most of these pupils had not coped well in a mainstream class, failing to interact with peers and doing little work without individual attention from the teacher. In these preparatory periods, they were not only provided with a preview of the planned topic for the week but were also given practice in the exercise of those inter-personal skills which would be required of them. This was held to be especially relevant to drama and RE, where pupils had found group work, class discussion and reporting back to the class particularly difficult to achieve. They had experienced additional problems with listening comprehension skills. The extra lesson each week gave practice in all of these skills and assisted considerably in the subsequent success of pupils' integration.

In one school with visually impaired pupils on roll, a variation on the preparation of pupils took place. Here, all staff involved in teaching maths to a blind pupil met together once a week in order to plan the following week's work. These timetabled meetings usually involved the specialist teacher, the ancillary and the class teacher. It was considered essential that the specialist teacher be given time to prepare work in braille and also, from time to time, to arrange for the purchase and use of other tactile teaching aids. All the staff in question found this to be a satisfactory way of cooperating over the maths education of their blind students.

Specialist or alternative tuition provided during lesson time

In some schools, specialist help was made available during part or all of a given lesson, so that a pupil with special needs could receive assistance as required. Details of these support schemes are given in chapters 7 and 13, where the help provided by classroom ancillaries, support teachers and by other pupils is explored. It should also be remembered in this context that many mainstream teachers will have planned and resourced their lessons bearing in mind the varying and individual special needs of pupils in the group, and that they will be aware of the most appropriate teaching strategies to adopt in order to maximize opportunities for all to participate. Chapters 10, 11 and 12 focus on these aspects of pedagogy.

However, there are some special needs which may still require input from a source outside the classroom, and in some schools arrangements were made so that pupils could go elsewhere to receive extra or alternative teaching and then return to the classroom. The programmes we observed made it clear just how important a cooperative teaching style and good working relationships between the class teacher and the support team were to the success of this kind of scheme. As with pre-lesson support, it was necessary for the specialist or support staff to have knowledge of the lesson topic(s) so that the most appropriate additional teaching could be given. Subject teachers in turn needed information about the kind of support being provided.

There is a danger in this situation that mainstream staff will feel that they are 'failing' in some way if a pupil leaves the classroom to be taught by someone else for a period of time. They must be helped to realize that the mainstream teaching they provide is not always appropriate for pupils with special needs. (Equally, pupils have to accept that they sometimes need a different medium or alternative teaching strategy in order to learn as efficiently as possible.) One helpful way of easing the anxiety that teachers sometimes felt was to arrange for discussion of the intervention being made and the reasons for it.

For example, a radio broadcast can pose problems for a hearing impaired pupil, while a television programme or film might present difficulty for a pupil with visual impairment, so these pupils are likely to benefit from receiving extra help in interpreting and understanding such audio-visual material. Providing this support within the class can be intrusive for other pupils and can also single out pupils in an unwelcome way. A brief period of withdrawal to view or to listen to the same material in company with a specialist helper can give a pupil both the information and the confidence needed in order to participate fully in the ensuing mainstream lesson.

The way in which this kind of special help was offered differed in primary and secondary sectors. Younger pupils were withdrawn for short periods of additional help when teachers deemed this to be necessary. As a rule pupils in primary schools used different resource materials at these times, but concepts were reinforced and skills developed which were relevant to the classroom topic and closely related to the pupil's level of development. Withdrawal was rarely for longer than 15 or 20 minutes at a time, and the pupil was thus able to return to class before a lesson or topic ended.

In programmes which were designed to support pupils whose problems manifested themselves both socially and academically, the provision of short periods of specialist help on a regular basis was seen as a helpful means of meeting their needs. For many of these younger pupils, a short period of withdrawal for specialist help by a staff member who was aware of the pupil's level of conceptual development and who could also see the problems faced in a mainstream setting was considered particularly advantageous.

At secondary level it was most common for a pupil to leave the mainstream classroom in order to use specialist equipment elsewhere for a short period. Generally pupils were expected to decide for themselves just when they needed extra help or the use of an alternative teaching mode, and our observations showed that they responded well to the opportunities offered. For example, in one school pupils would visit the resources area in order to use the closed circuit TV which enabled them to read an enlarged version of the class text, or to use sloping drawing boards upon which their work could be anchored firmly under a suitable light source. In another school, pupils would sometimes leave the class in order to type or dictate answers in a test situation.

Two aspects of this provision at secondary level deserve mention. First, some older secondary pupils had initially resisted the idea of leaving the class when the option was first presented to them, since it marked them out as being different. The way in which the opportunity is presented to older pupils is very important, and some counselling may be necessary before a pupil can appreciate the difference which this extra help can make. Secondly, the way in which the secondary programmes were arranged meant that supervision rather than teaching help was what was generally required. To this extent these programmes were less demanding of teacher time, though there was still of course need for constant monitoring and supervisory support.

Post-lesson or back-up teaching

This proved to be the most usual kind of supplementary teaching provided for pupils with special needs, with tuition given on an individual or occasionally small group basis as a follow-up to mainstream lessons. This provision has implications for staff deployment and liaison, for the curriculum and for timetabling. Ideally, it was desirable if the teacher who provided help in the mainstream could also carry out subsequent back-up teaching as part of a continuous support programme, but this kind of continuity was rarely possible to organize because of the high level of staffing it required. Back-up support was most usually provided by specialist or ancillary staff, who relied on information from both the mainstream teacher and the pupil in order to guide them. The most useful information required of the mainstream teacher concerned content, resources and subject-specific vocabulary, but time did not always permit the exchange of this kind of information. Support teachers thus relied heavily on the pupil to supply the questions and pose the problems. The usual pattern was to work closely with individual pupils, discussing the mainstream lesson, ascertaining what had been covered, reinforcing concepts, revising vocabulary and checking that the content had been fully and correctly understood.

This form of supplementary teaching gave staff a valuable opportunity to check that pupils had understood the main points of the lesson and were able to make proper use of resource materials provided. Pupils with sensory impairment in particular were encouraged to explain what they had been doing during the lesson in order to find out how much they had understood, since these pupils are often hesitant to ask for help in the mainstream class. Supplementary teaching time with a well known member of staff, frequently in a familiar teaching area, gave the pupil the confidence to ask questions of a specialist in an individual or small group situation. This did much to boost confidence for future mainstream occasions, when it might be necessary for a pupil to ask questions in class. For some pupils, most notably those who were physically handicapped or had

severe sensory handicaps, the extra time provided by back-up
teaching gave them the opportunity to catch up and in this way
to maintain a pace and progress similar to that of mainstream
peers. The curricular areas for which back-up teaching was most
commonly organized were those traditionally regarded as academic subjects, i.e. English, maths, science and humanities. In
these subject areas failure to grasp a new concept could place a
pupil at a particular disadvantage. Reinforcement of new
vocabulary, revision of a mainstream learning sequence and a
review of the concepts covered soon after the mainstream lesson
were all helpful forms of support. Care was necessary, however,
to ensure that the supplementary teaching did not prevent the
pupil from attending other key lessons; it was essential to view
the pupil's entire curriculum as a whole, as well as the daily
pattern, so that imbalance could be avoided. The examples
which follow illustrate some of the ways in which back-up
teaching was organized for pupils with special needs.

In one secondary school most back-up lessons took place in
that part of the day which was timetabled for French, as only
rarely did hearing impaired pupils take a second language.
English and maths were taught in the partially hearing unit
where the specialist teacher was well acquainted with pupils'
progress in basic skills as well as their grasp of concepts.
Mainstream work was brought to this unit, where the teacher
checked over what had been done in class each day and focused
attention on homework tasks, ensuring that these were properly
understood and that the pupil was equipped to carry them out.
This specialist teacher stressed the importance of maintaining
regular liaison with subject staff, so that she could learn more
about the subject matter covered in order to alert the subject
teacher to possible problem areas in the syllabus.

Timetabling influenced arrangements in another secondary
school, where a physically handicapped pupil required considerable additional time in which to dictate notes, for example, or
type up classwork. In addition to receiving classroom support in
the form of a welfare assistant, the pupil's timetable was
structured to give several periods of non-teaching time each
week, in which she could complete written notes and assignments in her own time and at her own pace. This had the effect

of increasing the pupil's confidence noticeably over the three terms during which our research was conducted at the school.

A school in which pupils with specific learning difficulties were catered for was using material from class lessons in a specialist unit in order to give pupils practice in writing and spelling words with which they had problems. It was planned in the future to liaise with subject departments and to prepare pupils beforehand by providing them with key subject-specific words to learn and practise. However, at the time of our visit specialist work in the unit consisted of revision, review and practice writing.

Another secondary school with several hearing impaired pupils who were following examination courses provided a very flexible back-up system. For example, the head of the special unit liaised with the science teacher in order to provide back-up support in physics for a boy who took three out of four options, spending the extra time in the partial hearing unit receiving support in science and in any other subjects with which he had difficulty. Another pupil spent approximately two periods each week in the unit, talking through assignments since her physical disability made writing a very slow process. One sixth former spent two or three lessons per week in the unit, talking through abstract concepts which she found particularly difficult. In-class support for this girl had previously been tried but rejected, as she felt that undue attention was being drawn to her, and the staff involved were agreeable to seeking an alternative form of back-up support; as the teacher in charge explained, staff could give individual attention to a pupil in the unit and explain the technical language of a subject in a way which was not possible during a class lesson.

Pre-lesson and post-lesson support

In a small number of schools the effort was made to provide support before *and* after lessons in an integrated way. As well as giving pupils the benefits of both preparatory and follow-up work, this arrangement capitalized on the time devoted to supplementary teaching: the two aspects could be closely related not only to the intervening lesson(s) but to each other as well. It was of course expensive in terms of staff time, both in providing such a high level of additional support and engaging in the necessary consultation and planning.

The pre- and post-lesson support paradigm took different forms in different schools, but was considered particularly desirable for basic skills and for areas such as maths where learning was perceived to be sequential. Our research would suggest also that it is best reserved for pupils of secondary age, where a subject-focused curriculum can present pupils with specific difficulties. The pupil has to take considerable responsibility for his or her own learning and indicate when any part of the work to be done is not clear. Younger children are often not aware of the limitations in their understanding and are not so ready to ask for assistance.

An example of this form of support comes from a school where a deaf fifth year pupil previewed films and filmstrips which were used in lead lessons. The humanities department worked in teams and introduced each new topic with an audio-visual presentation made to several classes at once. It was not always possible in this situation to check what the deaf pupil had understood, and so the humanities teacher took time during the lunch hour to run through the presentations and discuss them with the pupil. Follow-up work was done by the specialist teacher of the deaf, who checked that this pupil had understood the lesson fully and knew what was required of him in the way of assignments and homework. This specialist attended all lead lessons, and emphasized the necessity of establishing and maintaining close liaison with the subject teacher.

This example highlights the importance of close consultation between specialist and mainstream staff at every stage of an integration programme: from the planning stage when content, materials and methodologies are first discussed, through the teaching stage when special resources or support mechanisms are often required, and on to the review and evaluation stage when assessments of pupils' achievements are made. The subject teacher and the specialist teacher have much to learn from one another, and by working together they can tailor a learning programme to the developing and changing needs of the pupil.

Chapter 4
Timetabling

For a school's timetable to accommodate the requirements of pupils with a wide range of special needs, considerable flexibility is required in terms of staff deployment, pupil grouping and curricular organization. The timetable is an enabling device in the sense that it provides the framework within which resources can be mobilized for specific purposes. From our visits to schools it has been possible to identify certain elements of timetabling which appear to facilitate the progress of integration, as well as some which constrain it.

Pupil grouping has already been considered in some detail in chapter 2. Here it is pertinent to recall that pupils with special needs could with benefit be placed in different kinds of mainstream settings; a pupil could be 'matched' with a set which was moving at an appropriate pace for a given subject. Both subject and specialist teachers in the secondary sector stressed that a pupil should integrate for the whole of a subject and not for one or two lessons a week. Pupils placed in mixed ability classes were likely to remain with the same group for most if not all areas of the curriculum, enabling friendships to develop. Timetabling was easy to arrange since an integrating pupil joined a specific class, and the balance of time in and out of this class could easily be altered to meet the pupil's needs.

A number of secondary schools organized mixed ability teaching groups in the entry year, and it was common for such groupings to continue in subsequent years, particularly for practical areas of the curriculum. Frequently, these were the curricular areas in which pupils with special needs were first integrated, so that teachers could observe their interaction with others and their competence in both social and academic skills. Where a pupil was perceived to be adjusting well to the new situation, an extension of the time spent in mainstream was usually considered on a subject-by-subject basis.

One secondary school, aware of the slower pace at which many of the pupils with learning difficulties and physical handicaps worked, had organized a series of 'half options' for 4th and 5th year pupils. These were courses with a practical bias, such as car maintenance and parentcraft, which did not lead to an external certificate. Groups were small and tasks were carefully structured.

In several schools the importance of scheduling sufficient back-up time with specialist staff was emphasized. Many pupils with special needs are known to work more slowly than other pupils and thus require more time to complete set tasks. Especially when they first joined mainstream lessons, it was considered vital to arrange sufficient time for specialist staff to check the work covered in mainstream lessons in order to identify and resolve any problems arising. It was stated on several occasions that pupils were often hesitant to ask for help in new and unfamiliar surroundings, and so both in-class support and back-up teaching were especially important in the early stages of integration.

Timetabling considerations affect the provision of back-up teaching, since at a suitable time not too long after the mainstream lesson a mainstream staff member or ancillary must be free at the same time as the pupil so that they can work together. Other factors such as pupil concentration and fatigue must be taken into account. For example, it is not ideal to follow up a lengthy academic lesson immediately with a period of intensive back-up support, especially if this occurs toward the end of the day.

In-class support was considered essential in a number of schools catering for pupils with special needs. Before a pupil joined a mainstream group it was first ascertained that specialist staff or ancillary help would be available, and then the pupil's timetable was written out by the teacher in charge in order that the pattern of support required was clearly shown, together with the proportion of mainstream/specialist teaching received. Arranging the timetables of support staff and tailoring this into the school's timetable could, and did, present problems in some situations where there were too few staff to cover all mainstream lessons. In these cases, there were a number of alternative approaches which were employed.

a) In some schools, the teacher in charge of pupils with special needs visited the classrooms to check on individual pupils' progress and to discuss any problems with the mainstream teacher. (This meant that the teacher in charge had to have a considerable amount of non-teaching time.)

b) When an ancillary was not required by a pupil throughout a lesson, she was released to assist other pupils, so that one ancillary supported several pupils with special needs.

c) Two pupils integrated together. This was found to be a helpful strategy, particularly at secondary level, since the pupils could give each other moral support in those lessons where a second teacher was not present. It should be stressed that this strategy worked most successfully with older pupils and it was only adopted where a support teacher was unavailable for one or two of the mainstream lessons.

Back-up teaching was a feature of both primary and secondary schools. In the primary sector, pupils were generally withdrawn on an individual basis after consultation with the class teacher to ensure that no vital part of the daily programme would be missed during the 20 minutes or so for which pupils were commonly absent. It was usual for a pupil to receive extra help several times a week, if not daily, and the times were deliberately varied so that a pupil did not miss the same activity each time. Essentially the teacher providing the back-up support organized her/his own timetable around the needs of the pupils.

In secondary schools, back-up teaching was more formalized in the sense that it took place at a scheduled time and on specific days. The timetabling of these arrangements was clear-cut: pupils had periods of back-up teaching built into the curriculum and these appeared on individual pupil timetables. A common tactic was to timetable back-up lessons for hearing impaired pupils during foreign language lessons, as these pupils did not usually take a foreign language, while some pupils with physical handicaps received physiotherapy during PE time. (There was a tendency for staff to assume too readily that certain pupils would not benefit from conventional PE lessons, even if modified appropriately.) Pupils with visual handicap and those with moderate learning difficulties were less easy to provide for on a similar timetabled basis, since their need for extra help tended to vary depending on the nature of the topics being taught. In one school, for example, maths was found to present particular difficulties for a blind pupil, and so one extra back-up lesson was provided for her each week, when she was given individual tuition. In another school a group of pupils who had behaviour problems were timetabled for an additional lesson each week, in which they learned to relate to a number of adults and became accustomed to working as members of a group.

The integrated day common in several primary schools was found to pose some problems of timetabling. While mainstream staff welcomed the flexibility the integrated day afforded in organizing individual pupil programmes, it could make the task of special needs support staff more difficult, since scheduled withdrawal for individual teaching, testing or physiotherapy or indeed off-site activities such as riding or swimming might well come at an inconvenient time in the pupil's daily activities. This problem, of which teachers were very aware, was best solved by close co-operation so that staff could tailor activities around the known fixed appointments.

In one primary school, the staff worked together in a different way to ensure that all pupils with special needs were receiving appropriate attention. On a roll of over 400 there were pupils with moderate learning difficulties, visual and hearing impairments, mild physical handicaps and emotional problems. One staff member was responsible for organizing the remedial back-up and welfare support given to each mixed ability class. Remedial help, physiotherapy and speech therapy were all timetabled, and three teachers co-ordinated the support programmes for pupils with special needs in reception/middle infants, top infants/first year juniors and middle/upper juniors respectively. Once a week part-time staff released each of the co-ordinators so that they could observe pupils, carry out testing, see parents or meet other class teachers to discuss pupils' progress. The main school building was largely open-plan and movement of adults through the different teaching areas was easy to arrange. Teachers and pupils were used to having ancillaries, physiotherapists, speech therapists, parents and part-time remedial teachers working alongside them or withdrawing a pupil for a period of time, and support was provided with a minimum of fuss to a large number of pupils who had very different educational needs. While this arrangement required a fairly high level of staffing, it was considered to pay dividends in the opportunities it provided for diagnosing individual needs, making provision to meet them and monitoring progress.

Where a school had links with outside agencies and with other schools, it was important for visits to be timetabled so that staff and pupils knew who was receiving help from whom, and also where the teaching was taking place. This meant that peripatetic staff did not lose valuable teaching time and mainstream teachers knew when a pupil would not be present in class. In one scheme, where pupils from a special school were attending some lessons in a nearby comprehensive school, the special school altered its daily timetable pattern to fit in with the timetable at the host school. This involved quite major changes, such as holding assembly at the end of the day instead of at the beginning and altering the times of breaks and lunch.

In general, meeting special educational needs in the ordinary school introduces a further level of complexity into the school's timetabling procedures. Where the latter are already complex, as in many secondary schools, this can pose considerable problems. Arrangements for special needs may have to take their place along with other arrangements, and the most that can be achieved is an uneasy compromise between what is desirable and what is feasible in practice. Some schools found that the timetable restructuring they sought could not be achieved in one academic year and had to be spread over several years. A key factor in most cases was the availability of 'surplus' staff: where support and staffing levels were only barely adequate there was little flexibility; where by contrast staffing levels were generous, individual arrangements could be accommodated far more readily.

Part Two
Modification to Curriculum Content

Chapter 5
Models of Curriculum Content

Curriculum models

The curriculum for pupils with special needs should be viewed in conjunction with the organization of the school, as this often determines whether a special or modified curriculum can be offered. As a parallel to the organizational provision, the curricular provision found in mainstream schools can also be seen as a continuum from full participation in the mainstream school curriculum to a special curriculum which bears little relationship to that being followed by age peers. Such a continuum could be summarized as:

1. Mainstream curriculum
2. Mainstream curriculum with some modification
3. Mainstream curriculum with significant modification
4. Special curriculum with addition
5. Special curriculum.

An alternative way of categorizing curricular variation is implied in the 1983 DES guidelines for completing forms 7 and 7M. (These are experimental and may be modified in the future.)
   i) Mainstream plus support: A curriculum as provided in ordinary schools but with the provision of additional support to pupils, which may be in the form of additional resoures, e.g. aids, small group teaching, ancillary help.
  ii) Modified: A curriculum similar to that provided in ordinary schools, but while not restricted in its expectations has objectives more appropriate to pupils with

moderate learning difficulties. This will include those previously categorized as ESN(M) (Educationally Sub-Normal (Moderate)).

iii) Developmental: A curriculum covering a range of educational experiences but more selectively and sharply focused on the development of personal autonomy and social skills, with precisely defined objectives, and designed for pupils with severe learning difficulties. This will include those previously categorized as ESN(S).

A rough correspondence can be drawn between the two sets of categories:

DES   i) and our 1
DES ii) and our 2 and 3
DES iii) and our 4 and 5.

The type of curriculum on offer, although determined largely by the organizational structure, also depended on the needs of the pupils being identified. Whether or not a pupil was perceived to have a special educational need was sometimes predetermined in that the pupil had been assessed as such by the LEA. In other cases, the pupils' needs were identified by the school's own testing procedures or came to notice as a result of the lack of expected progress.

1. *Mainstream curriculum*

The provision that was most likely to be made available to pupils with special needs was that in which they followed the same programmes of work in the same teaching groups as their peers. The reason usually given for the emphasis on the mainstream school curriculum was that pupils with special needs were only accepted on roll if they could cope intellectually with the existing mainstream curriculum. This was especially so in the case of physically handicapped pupils, but was also true in the case of some visually and hearing impaired pupils. However, it was noticeable that much effort was made, by way of teaching arrangements and support, to help such pupils cope with and participate fully in the school's mainstream curriculum. The various approaches used are discussed in later chapters.

The other models of curriculum content entailed a departure from the mainstream curriculum to a greater or lesser extent. Whether the curriculum was modified to any degree reflected the organizational structure of the school. The main reasons given for modification were twofold:

    i) there was a need for some specialist teaching in areas causing difficulty;

    ii) there were subject areas thought to be unsuitable for the stage reached by the pupil, and the time could be better used for other areas.

A modified curriculum was generally biased to individual pupils and reflected their particular strengths and weaknesses. Indeed, many pupils required some form of specialist teaching geared to their learning difficulties. There appeared to be a fine balance between offering programmes of work related to pupils' special needs and ensuring that the curriculum did not become a separatist device cutting off pupils with special needs from their age peers. Mainstream teachers saw little point in resolving a pupil's learning difficulties by means of a specialized curriculum if this made it more difficult for the pupil to establish contact with age peers and participate fully in the social environment. They would rather try to resolve learning difficulties within a mainstream setting whenever possible.

2. *Mainstream curriculum with some modification*

The majority of pupils following a modified curriculum carried out essentially the same work as their age peers with similar expectations but having objectives more appropriate to pupils concerned. This involved omitting some topic or subject areas and replacing them by supplementary and alternative activities related to individual pupils' needs. For example, it was essential that some visually handicapped pupils learned typing or braille; likewise some physically handicapped pupils needed to learn skills which compensated for motor deficiencies. Sometimes it was necessary to devise individual programmes of work in given subject areas, particularly for pupils with learning difficulties.

    If it was necessary for alternative programmes to be implemented on a withdrawal basis most schools tried to ensure this was done to give minimal disruption to the mainstream timetable. The advantage of offering a modified curriculum of this sort lay in its flexibility. Some of the required modifications which compensated for gaps in knowledge or basic training that would otherwise interfere with future learning were only temporarily required. Such modifications may only be required at an early age, and the pupil may be able to cope with a full mainstream curriculum in later school years. For example, the emphasis on speech development for the hearing impaired pupil in primary school may not be necessary by the time the pupil reaches secondary level.

3. *Mainstream curriculum with significant modification*

The emphasis here was still on making available as much of the mainstream curriculum as possible, but taking greater account of pupils' individual needs and capacities. This entailed modifying the mainstream curriculum to a greater or lesser extent, usually in the context of a unit base or a significant amount of withdrawal from mainstream lessons. These arrangements were usually made in favour of pupils with moderate learning difficulties or those with severe hearing loss.

The most common pattern was to supplement mainstream English and maths with additional work on a withdrawal basis or, alternatively, to provide language and number work on an entirely separate basis. Other subjects were taken as part of a mainstream group, though with considerable variation in practice from school to school. Depending on how much additional time was given over to literacy and numeracy, some subjects were dropped or given less time and attention. Thus hearing impaired pupils, particularly at primary level, may require a large part of their timetable to be given over to speech and language development. Physically handicapped pupils may need to spend time in activities such as swimming and horse riding or receiving physiotherapy and speech therapy.

As these additional activities are necessary to the pupils' overall development, the timetable followed will reflect the school's attempts to meet these individual needs. As a result, the curriculum on offer to these pupils may appear significantly modified when compared to that being followed by peers. It is important however to maintain sufficient flexibility to enable pupils with special needs to extend into other areas of the mainstream curriculum as their requirement of specialized intervention diminishes.

4. *Special curriculum with additions*

The emphasis here was on pupils' special needs and, while the curriculum might cover a range of educational experiences, its primary definition was in terms of how these pupils were different from their peers, rather than what they had in common with them. The starting point in curriculum development was individual needs, and only when these were seen to be met was consideration given to the parts of the mainstream curriculum that could then be made available. In operational terms this resulted in a heavy concentration on basic work in language and number, with extension into other curricular areas having secondary importance. This concentration on the basics did sometimes lead to pupils following a narrow programme of work, a fact which highlights the importance of modifying the curriculum so that pupils have access to a wide range of subject areas and have as balanced a curriculum content as possible.

5. *Special curriculum*

This was rare, as it was only offered to pupils when taught entirely in special classes or units. In these cases, priority was given to ensuring that pupils had an adequate grounding in basic subjects – reading, writing and mathematics. In addition, there was usually a focus on the development of personal autonomy and social skills, with precisely defined objectives. Most of the pupils involved were within the ESN(S) (Educationally Sub-Normal (Severe)) range.

In such units or classes pupils spent more time with one teacher (usually a unit/class teacher) than was usual for age peers in mainstream classes. This was particularly noticeable at secondary level, where other pupils were moving between several teachers for the different subject areas. The advantage to the group of a single teacher was in the positive manner of recording progress and achievement and in the continuity of teaching achieved. The disadvantage was in the considerable segregation such a special curriculum imposed on the pupils concerned.

Many unit/class teachers questioned the advisability of a totally special curriculum on the grounds that there could be adverse effects on the progress and development of their pupils because of the reduced exposure to the stimulation of age peers. Other negative effects were thought to be a lowering of pupil aspirations and teacher expectations, causing a further restriction of the curriculum.

Access to the curriculum

Access to the mainstream curriculum, in part or in total, depends on the organization within the school. Other factors which come into play as far as the individual pupil is concerned are individual pupil needs, teacher availability, subject content and physical barriers.

If a programme of work is to be designed to meet the needs of an individual pupil, the needs of the pupil must first be identified. The processes schools used in identifying individual needs were wide-ranging. Some schools depended on the information given on SE (Special Education) forms, although many teachers were conscious that much of the medical and social history given in them had little or no relevance to the pupils' educational needs. In this respect the new assessment procedures required by the 1981 Education Act should help to ensure that schools have relevant information, at least on those pupils for whom a Statement of educational needs has been made.

Many schools preferred to supplement information obtained about pupils with special needs with information from their own diagnostic and assessment procedures. This assessment was carried out in the special unit or classes if these were on site or in the mainstream class after an initial settling down period. Those schools with special units/classes on site were noticeably more precise and organized in their initial diagnosis and assessment procedures than schools where pupils with special needs were based in mainstream classes. Naturally, the former were more likely to have specialist staff well qualified and experienced in assessing pupils with special needs. Assessment from a mainstream class base was often in terms of an overall judgement as to whether the pupil was coping or not.

In schools with special units/classes on site the usual procedure was for a pupil to spend the first few weeks at the school in the unit/class full-time. This initial period enabled staff to get to know the pupil, observe the pupil at work and carry out any necessary testing. Most staff emphasized the importance of competence in basic academic and social skills when considering access to the mainstream curriculum, particularly at primary school level. At secondary level a pupil's aptitude for and attitude to particular curricular areas were emphasized.

An example of an assessment procedure used by a unit for partially hearing pupils is given. This unit, based within a secondary school, has on roll some profoundly deaf pupils. Its aim is maximum involvement of unit pupils in the mainstream curriculum. The procedure exemplified is typical of that used by many other units in assessing their pupils.

Assessment of a pupil based on ATTITUDE and APTITUDE

These two categories should be investigated carefully before any pupil is integrated into theoretical (language biased) subjects.

Standard practice is for immediate integration into practical subjects, including Craft and PE.

Immediate 23 per cent integration. Careful monitoring required at all times.

Initial Diagnosis Prior to Full-time Education at . . . .

INTERVIEW
1. Whether pupil pays heed to discussion between PHU (Partial
   Hearing Unit) Staff, Main
   School Staff, parents, guardians
   or any such person who attends
   the interview   . . . .
2. Makes an attempt to under-
   stand PHU Staff or relies on
   others for interpretation or
   guidance   . . . .
3. Shows an interest in his/her
   future   . . . .
4. Volunteers to communicate (if
   only to say hello and goodbye)   . . . .
5. Shows an interest in surroun-
   dings and other pupils of the
   PHU and Main School   . . . .
6. Wearing Hearing Aids and
   attitude to them   . . . .

ATTITUDE: SUB-CATEGORIES
1. Personality   2. Character
(a) inter-relationships with
      (i) Hearing peers
      (ii) Hearing Impaired peers
(b) confident
(c) responsible
(d) ambitious/competitive
(e) expressive, demonstrative
(f) adaptable
(g) has a sense of humour
School psychologist's assessment.

APTITUDE: SUB-CATEGORIES
1. Previous school's assessment
   and tests   . . . .
2. Lip-reading ability   . . . .

3. Motor control and manual dexterity . . . .
4. Observation potential* . . . .
5. Imagination and ability to express that imagination . . . .
6. Discussion potential . . . .
7. Response and reaction to humour . . . .
8. Instructional response (comprehension)* . . . .
9. Conceptual understanding . . . .
10. Reasoning ability . . . .
11. Willingness to attempt new concepts and projects . . . .
12. Memory and ability to assimilate, retain and apply (numerical order, syntactical order, etc.) . . . .
13. Logics . . . .
14. Social awareness* . . . .
15. Initiative . . . .
16. Interest, subject interest and preference . . . .

As educationalists, Aptitude assessments are our main concern, though we acknowledge that the two are inseparable.

EXPLANATION OF SUB-CATEGORIES*
4. Observation potential – definite use of the visual sense.
8. Instructional response – comprehension of instructions and directions.
14. Social awareness – knowledge of current affairs, manners etc.

Naturally we do not expect the pupil to fulfil all these sub-categories during the diagnostic period.

After selected integration the programme of education will be to develop these skills, and assessment should be made periodically.

LENGTH OF DIAGNOSTIC TIME
Approximately
1) 5 weeks; 2) 3 months; 3) annually; 4) finally.

Teacher availability affected curricular access in several ways. Sometimes, particularly in academic subjects, there were too few mainstream teachers available. Schools tried to avoid over-loading classes or subject areas, allowing for one or two pupils with special needs per class. This was a particular problem at one primary school having on roll a large number of pupils with a variety of special needs. A greater number of pupils could have benefited from access to the mainstream had more staff been available. Many schools stressed the importance of maintaining the goodwill of mainstream staff, implying that their efforts in this regard were a significant limiting factor.

Some pupils could follow mainstream lessons if additional help was made available to them, for example, in follow-up work with specialist teachers. This form of support has been described in chapter 3. However it is provided, it is expensive in teacher time and not always possible.

Occasionally access to a curricular area was achieved by placing the pupil with special needs in a lower ability group since such groups were generally smaller in number. This was not always a satisfactory solution particularly when the pupil concerned was of high ability.

The handicapping conditions of many pupils had led to their spending considerable time reaching a basic competence in literacy and numeracy. Attention then switched to subject areas less dependent on literacy, such as the practical areas of art, craft, PE and music in order to try to balance their programme of work. Constraints, such as prior know-ledge of a subject area or the pace at which it is taught, which were used by many schools to decide on the curricular areas to be made available to pupils with special needs, may not be so important as previously considered. Motivation and aptitude of the pupil for a particular subject area may be more important, as suggested below.

In many subject areas where knowledge and understanding are cumulative it is generally regarded as essential that access to them has to be made at an early stage. Difficulties can arise when a pupil takes on such a subject area part way through a course because some essential knowledge given earlier on is missing. However some schools have successfully opened up such curricular areas to pupils with special needs by relying on pupils' aptitude and interest in that area, rather than the amount of knowledge previously acquired. For example, one profoundly deaf pupil was able to take up an examination course in mathematics although she had missed significant parts of the course taught previously. Her aptitude and motivation for the subject countered any deficiencies in knowledge, and with some extra help she was soon able to acquire the necessary factual information to cope with the course.

The pace at which some subject areas were taught and the depth to which they were considered may be a problem for some pupils, particularly those with learning problems. It was found, however, that the way in which material was presented could help such pupils cope with much more than was previously thought possible. One school, catering for several pupils with moderate learning difficulties, ensured that each new topic in any subject was approached from the concrete level, with pupils encouraged to manipulate materials. In this way, it was found that essential basic concepts could be understood and used by the pupils as the topic was covered in greater depth. Such an approach was also helpful to many other pupils, ensuring sounder understanding of new work without detracting from the pace at which the work had to be covered.

Access to the curriculum was sometimes limited on account of inaccessibility of parts of the school to some pupils. This was a particular problem for physically handicapped pupils. Schools did try to circumvent physical barriers to ensure open access to all parts of the curriculum; in some cases this meant rearranging the timetable, swapping rooms for those more accessible to the pupil. Those steps did not of course resolve the problem of rooms having to be used which were inappropriate to the subject, too small or lacking appropriate resources. One school dealt with the problem of limited accessibility to upstairs rooms by rearranging the groups to which the physically handicapped pupil belonged. Several subjects (art, music and RE) were all in upstairs rooms so the pupil joined a different form group for these subjects in order to spend complete mornings in these upstairs rooms.

The above examples and the achievements of individual schools in opening up the mainstream curriculum to pupils with special needs underlines the importance of re-examining ideas and concepts about the curriculum for these pupils. Instead of dwelling on the constraints associated with some subject areas, the emphasis should be more on a pupil's own aptitude and motivation for particular subjects. No areas of the curriculum should be automatically ruled out of consideration for pupils with special needs, and the resulting curricular offerings may provide a more satisfactory balance for pupil and teachers alike.

Chapter 6
Individual Programmes
of Work

The range of curricular provision outlined in the previous chapter was reflected in the diversity of individual pupils' learning experiences. Formal programmes of work are only part of a pupil's total curricular experience. Classroom practice, interaction with peers and the non-formal activities subsumed under the 'hidden curriculum' are all major components of the learning process in schools. The individual timetable, however, with its associated programme of work, provides a visible indication of how a school is modifying its curriculum for given pupils.

The purpose of this chapter therefore is to describe individual programmes of work drawn from a number of schools. These have been selected to exemplify three of the curricular models described above. These examples also highlight the degree of flexibility achieved by some schools in meeting the needs of pupils and illustrate the range of activities undertaken by pupils with special needs in mainstream settings.

Mainstream curriculum with some modification

Our first example is the programme of work followed by a visually impaired pupil in a large primary school. This school is partially open plan and works a form of integrated day. (As can be seen from the timetable, numeracy and literacy tend to be taught in the morning and the practical subjects in the afternoon.) The topic work includes a wide range of subject areas and is used to increase language experience through writing and reading. In addition, two half-periods are devoted to language. The pupil was in his fourth year and followed the same timetable as his peers with two exceptions (example 1). To compensate for his visual loss he was given additional teaching in visual discrimination and reading skills and was also learning braille. The time needed for these additional activities was gained by omitting craft and practical science. These were chosen because they were felt to be areas of least benefit to the pupil at this time and because some science was covered in topic work.

At the same school a pupil with moderate learning difficulties was following a similar timetable. She was withdrawn for one period a week, in her case for one of the class language periods in order to engage in intensive language development work on an individual basis. Otherwise she joined all the curriculum activities of the group.

Modifications to timetables and programmes of work may also occur because of transport problems rather than to meet any educational need. However much it may be regretted on educational grounds, special transport required some pupils to leave school earlier than their peers. Schools concerned tended to counter this by timetabling these activities from which it was felt the pupil would gain least benefit at the end of the day. Thus a junior school pupil with cerebral palsy who was fully able to follow the mainstream curriculum had to leave school three-quarters of an hour early to catch special transport home. This meant she missed the last part of each day, with the exception of those days when parents were able to collect her. The teacher rearranged the class timetable so that all lessons at the end of the day were craft, games or PE.

At secondary level, modification of this kind often took the form of a slight narrowing of curriculum content. An entire subject area, especially second languages, might be dropped in order to give a pupil more time for work in other areas. Example 2 outlines the timetable followed by a second year physically handicapped pupil at a comprehensive school. French was dropped in order to make room for typing lessons – necessary so that she could cope with written assignments – and to provide two free periods when she could catch up on other subjects.

EXAMPLE 1
Mainstream curriculum with some modification

	MONDAY	TUESDAY	WEDNESDAY	THURSDAY	FRIDAY
9.00 13.30	*Maths*	*Maths*	*Maths*	*Maths*	*Maths*
	B	R	E	A	K
10.45 12.00	*Language* *Topic*	*Topic*	*Topic*	*Embroidery* *Topic*	*Topic*
	L	U	N	C	H
1.15 2.45 3.30	READING BRAILLE WRITING *Soccer*	*Swimming* *Topic*	*Language* *P.E.*	*Art* *Music*	VISUAL DISCRIMI- NATION WORK READING SKILLS

For all timetables, CAPITAL letters indicate when pupil is withdrawn for specialist help in unit area.
ITALIC letters indicate when pupil is working with mainstream class.

It will be noted that this pupil's timetable was modified in a further respect. The school had devised new 'developmental' courses in maths and language for its low-attaining pupils, and that for language was being followed by this pupil. The aims of the courses were given as
   1) to develop appreciation of the need for skills in literacy, numeracy and oracy
   2) to develop social and moral awareness
   3) to relate the pupil to his future role in society.
The courses were structured and contained a core element which was designed to enhance the development of basic concepts and skills in mathematics and literacy. A synopsis of the language course is given in example 3.

EXAMPLE 2
Mainstream curriculum with some modification

	MONDAY	TUESDAY	WEDNESDAY	THURSDAY	FRIDAY
1	Domestic	Biology	Art	Language	Needle-
2	Science	Biology	Art	Development	work
3	Maths	FREE	Biology	TYPING	Maths
4	L. Dev.	FREE	Music/RE	TYPING	L. Dev.
5	Geography	EPR	Swimming	History	Drama
6	Geography	EPR	Swimming	History	Games*
7	English	L. Dev.	Maths	English	Biology
8	English	Maths	Maths	English	Biology

L. Dev. = Language Development
Games* = Table tennis
Music/RE = alternate weeks
EPR = Education for Personal Relationships

EXAMPLE 3
Development Education – Language

The Language course embraces all aspects of literacy and oracy. The pupils should be encouraged to think for themselves, to use dictionaries and reference books freely and confidently. The object of the course is the positive development of the skilled use of written and spoken English enabling the pupil to communicate in all the necessary ways relevant to his/her future role in society.

Aural and Oral aspects of language

A list of general skills which could serve as a good background for further work in the IVth year.

(a) Listening skills
(b) Clear verbal expression of the pupil's thoughts and feelings
(c) Use of correct intonation (in using one's own language and in interpreting that of others)

(d) Giving and following instructions on simple tasks
(e) The ability to hold the attention of an audience by use of imaginative verbal skills
(f) The use of a variety of expressions and a rich vocabulary in speech
(g) Social skills.

As the course develops there may be additions to the list.

Content of syllabus – for structured written lessons (3 periods per week)

Abbreviations	Comprehension	Prepositions
Adjectives	Connecting words	Pronouns
Adverbs	Diminutives	(Direct) Speech
Alphabetical order	Formation of	marks
Apostrophe	adjectives	Verbs
–Contraction	Formation of nouns	Punctuation
–Possession		
Analogies	Group Names	Unusual Plurals
Capital letters	Homonyms	Double Negatives
Collective nouns	Homophones	Either, neither
Completing	Nouns – definition	Comparative
sentences	Occupations	Superlative
Composition of	Opposites	Fewer than –
sentences		less than

Resources
1. Individual tapes for pupils
2. Tape recorder
3. Video tapes.

In addition to the above core course there will be a double lesson for project work, drama, verbal expression work, etc. Here the major aim is to encourage the development of creative expression in Language by the pupil and to encourage self-discipline in carrying out his or her research in individual work with projects. Drama should encourage self awareness and confidence.

The policy at another secondary school, with a number of visually impaired pupils on roll, was that these pupils should do the same work as their peers, with modifications made as necessary. Thus, two blind pupils required additional time to keep up with academic work as well as time for training in mobility and daily living skills. To accommodate these needs, the academic load was reduced by one subject – again this was French – and instruction in braille was given at lunch time during the braille club meetings. The mobility training included the development of spatial concepts, body awareness, training in the use of other senses and the ability to move safely in both familiar and strange environments. Daily living skills included training in personal hygiene and grooming, selection of clothes, washing–up, ironing, kitchen safety and shopping. (On occasion it was necessary to teach the use of residual vision and visual discrimination skills to less severely visually impaired pupils. Such pupils normally followed the common timetable but were withdrawn for training as required).

Mainstream curriculum with significant modification

A significantly modified curriculum was most usually offered by schools with unit facilities and was most often required by pupils with severe hearing loss or moderate learning difficulties. Our first example relates to a profoundly deaf pupil at a comprehensive school with unit facilities on site, who was able to follow 60 per cent of the normal timetable, as illustrated in example 4. The work in the unit concentrated on literacy skills and language development, including some speech therapy. To maintain curricular balance, art and geography were also taught in the unit, following the mainstream curriculum. In addition, some back-up support work was given for science and history which were taught in the mainstream. Pupils with moderate learning difficulties require intensive help in basic skills. Their low levels of attainment may preclude them from examination subjects at secondary level but not from joining non-examination groups taking these subjects. A 4th year pupil with moderate learning difficulties was able to follow a range of subjects in the mainstream in this way (example 5).

EXAMPLE 4
Mainstream curriculum with significant modification

	1	2	3	4	5	6	7	8
MONDAY	*History*	PHU	PHU	L	PHU	PHU	*Maths*	PHU
TUESDAY	PHU	PHU	*PE*	U	*Craft*	*Craft*	*Maths*	PHU
WEDNESDAY	*Craft*	*Craft*	PHU	N	*History*	*Science*	*Science*	PHU
THURSDAY	*Maths*	*Maths*	*Science*	C	*PE*	*PE*	PHU	*Assembly*
FRIDAY	PHU	PHU	PHU	H	*PE*	*Science*	PHU	*Maths*

Lunch is 40 minutes only.
PHU = Partial Hearing Unit.

EXAMPLE 5
Mainstream curriculum with significant modification

	1	2	3	4	5		6	7	8
MONDAY	ENGLISH	MATHS	*Social Studies*	*Art*	*Art*	L	*Tutor Group*	ENGLISH	MATHS
TUESDAY	*Art*	*Art*	MATHS	ENGLISH	*Home Economics*	U	R I D I N G		
WEDNESDAY	*Community Service (playgroup)*		*Social Studies*	*Games*	*Games*	N	ENGLISH	MATHS	*Careers*
THURSDAY	*Art*	*Art*	*Religious Education*		ENGLISH	C	MATHS	*Parent Craft*	
FRIDAY	*Social Studies*		*Home Economics*		*Art*	H	*Art*	MATHS	ENGLISH

At another secondary school, pupils in the dyslexia unit had their academic load reduced by one subject, in that they were withdrawn from French, and followed a specialized maths and English programme in the unit. Mainstream maths was thought to be unsuitable for these pupils, at least until their third year. The unit had developed special strategies including relaxation at the beginning of each lesson and the use of computer games to develop spatial awareness, number sequencing and place value.

English was taught in the unit up to and including CSE Mode III with concessions for spelling. The rest of the timetable was identical to that of their peers.

Special curriculum with additions

A small number of pupils with severe and complex learning difficulties required highly specialized teaching. Individual special programmes were devised for them and implemented separately from mainstream classes. Such individual work tended to be carried out in a unit base, and focused on reading, oracy, writing and numeracy. Some pupils needed additional instruction in social and motor coordination skills, and possibly speech therapy or physiotherapy.

In order to minimize the effects of the curricular separation arising in this way, several schools arranged for some lessons to be taken in the mainstream. This was often in practical subject areas. For a few pupils, however, practical subjects presented great difficulty or lessons were too unstructured for them. In these cases efforts were sometimes made to enable them to join mainstream classes in other subjects for at least one or two lessons a week.

Another way of working toward curricular integration for these pupils was to establish a common core curriculum. This was seen as a way of making it easier to reduce the amount of time pupils were taught in a separate unit and increasing their time in the mainstream, since it established a measure of curricular continuity. Such a common core might include:

i) a common reading scheme but with additional resources for pupils with special needs

ii) a common approach to the teaching of skills such as handwriting

iii) a common approach to mathematical concepts with additional resources for pupils with special needs

iv) a linking curricular area such as topic or project work followed by the whole school.

Example 6 is the timetable of a pupil with severe physical and communication difficulties. This pupil enjoyed the company of

EXAMPLE 6
Special curriculum with additions

	MONDAY	TUESDAY	WEDNESDAY	THURSDAY	FRIDAY
8.55 9.30	*Assembly*	*Assembly*	SPEECH	*Assembly*	*Assembly*
	UNIT	*TV Words and pictures*	PHYSIO	UNIT	SPEECH
10.00	PHYSIO	UNIT	GROUP PHYSIO	UNIT	PE
10.30 10.45	B	R	E	A	K
	Music	SPEECH	UNIT	*Music*	PHYSIO
11.25			*Science*		
	SPEECH	UNIT	UNIT	UNIT	UNIT
12.00 1.15	L	U	N	C	H
	UNIT	*Writing and Story*	UNIT	TV 'Watch'	SWIMMING
	UNIT		SPEECH	SPEECH	
2.15 2.30	B	R	E	A	K
	RIDING	UNIT	REMEDIAL GROUP	*Follow up work 'Watch'*	UNIT
3.00 3.30		UNIT		LANGUAGE	UNIT

his non–handicapped peers and was able to join them for some TV programmes and associated work. (The school made extensive use of TV series.) This work enhanced his language development and encouraged his learning and use of Bliss symbols to communicate with peers. He was also able to join them for music, for which he showed a particular aptitude, but not for art or craft which he appeared to dislike and refused to do. Most of his time was spent in the unit following a programme on literacy and numeracy. One double period was spent with a small group of mainstream pupils who were judged to need extra specialist teaching. In addition, there was a double period of science taught in the unit by a mainstream teacher.

EXAMPLE 7
Special curriculum with additions

	MONDAY	TUESDAY	WEDNESDAY	THURSDAY	FRIDAY
8.55					
	Assembly	*Assembly*	UNIT	*Assembly*	*Assembly*
9.30					
	UNIT	UNIT	UNIT	UNIT	UNIT
10.00					
	UNIT	UNIT	PHYSIO	*PE*	UNIT
10.30					
	B	R	E	A	K
10.45					
	UNIT	UNIT	UNIT	UNIT	UNIT
11.25					
	UNIT	UNIT	UNIT	UNIT	UNIT
12.00					
	L	U	N	C	H
1.15					
	PE		*PE*		
1.45		REMEDIAL GROUP		*Craft*	SWIMMING
	TV progs		*TV and writing*		
2.15					
	B	R	E	A	K
2.30					
					UNIT
	Art	*Craft*	*Pottery*	REMEDIAL GROUP	
3.00					
					UNIT
3.30					

Example 7 presents the timetable for another pupil from the same unit. She had moderate learning difficulties and followed a broadly similar programme. She was particularly keen on practical subjects, however, and took art, craft and PE with mainstream groups.

Example 8 is the timetable for two pupils with severe learning difficulties based in a unit in a secondary school. Although all of their work was done in the unit, efforts were made to ensure mainstream contact. A number of subject teachers came to the unit to teach (times indicated by asterisk); this was a contributory factor in enabling these pupils to follow a relatively wide programme of work. Some mainstream pupils requiring intensive remedial support worked alongside these pupils for reading skills periods. In addition, of course, there was contact with mainstream peers at registration, break and lunchtime and in the course of club activities.

EXAMPLE 8
Special Need (SL): Timetable for pupils with severe learning difficulties: Special curriculum with additions

	1	2	3	4	5
MONDAY	ENVIRON-MENTAL STUDIES	READING SKILLS	MUSIC	CREATIVE WRITING COMPRE-HENSION*	READING GAMES AND SENSE TRAINING*
TUESDAY	IS SCRIPTURE	IS HISTORY	MATHS*	IS GEOGRAPHY*	ART
WEDNESDAY	HOME SKILLS	SOCIAL TRAINING (out doors) shops etc.	HOME SKILLS	DRAMA*	CRAFT*
THURSDAY	INTEGRATED	COMMUNI-CATION	SKILLS	PROJECTS/ ACTIVITIES*	MATHS
FRIDAY	LISTENING SKILLS	MATHS	STORIES/ GAMES	SCIENCE*	TABLE GAMES

* indicates lesson taught by mainstream teachers.

Summary

This chapter has shown some of the diverse ways in which schools modified the curriculum for pupils with special needs.

The diversity is inevitable, given the different needs of individual pupils and the different situations of the schools they attend; however, two important pointers for practice stand out. First, schools should not lose sight of curricular balance in seeking to meet pupils' special needs. In particular, literacy and numeracy must not so crowd the timetable that other subject areas cannot be taken seriously. Second, the mainstream curriculum must be borne in mind when individual programmes are being devised. Particularly if greater curricular integration is a possible target, it is important to relate special programmes to mainstream work and develop common threads where possible. As well as preparing pupils with special needs for greater mainstream involvement, this makes it possible to draw on mainstream curriculum resources and helps to make these pupils more truly a part of the school.

Part Three
Staffing

Chapter 7
Teachers, Ancillaries
and Liaison

A school's staff is its major resource. Coping effectively with special needs entails changing the roles and deployment of staff. This is especially significant both in respect of what we term designated teachers and also of ancillary staff. The issue of liaison, which assumes particular importance when many staff have dealings with individual pupils, is discussed here as well.

Staffing changes

The introduction of pupils with special needs, whether individually or unit based, has implications for school staffing levels and the criteria used to determine them. LEA policy on this matter seemed to be extremely variable and considerable differences were found in practice. It was generally acknowledged, however, that the demands of educating pupils with special needs in the mainstream necessitated changes in the staffing establishment of schools.

Some of the changes were achieved by relatively minor adjustments to the responsibilities of existing staff; others involved taking on new personnel and allocating quite new responsibilities. The staffing changes fell into four broad categories:
1. Increasing the role of mainstream staff
2. Increasing the staffing establishment of the school generally
3. Recruiting a full-time specialist teacher or teacher responsible for pupils with special needs
4. Increasing the ancillary allocation.

1.   *Extending the role of mainstream staff*

Many schools catering for pupils with special needs on an individual basis had little opportunity to acquire extra staff. Making provision for these pupils was simply an extra task for the head teacher and some staff. For the most part such pupils became the responsibility of the remedial department and any special help required was given by that department. Some remedial teachers welcomed this enhanced role since the increased responsibility often meant upgrading the department and giving it a more significant role within the school. Many staff however found the increased responsibilities extremely demanding. Some found it difficult to make the switch from working as individuals to working in a team context. Some teachers found themselves inundated with requests for help to the point where the assistance they could offer was superficial, or so belated that it was unappreciated or even criticized. In other situations the teacher or the department as a whole did not have the requisite expertise. When this occurred, the net result tended to be a loss of morale and negative reaction on the part of other staff.

In all schools visited in the project, the presence of pupils with special needs imposed demands on mainstream staff as the pupils observed were receiving at least half their education in mainstream classes. The ability of mainstream staff to cope depended on their own experience, training and knowledge of the special needs concerned. To meet these needs certain changes in classrooms and teaching had to be made, and additional time was taken up with monitoring pupil progress. These changes and new responsibilities are discussed in the section on Teaching.

2.   *Increasing the staffing complement of the school generally*

In order to cope with some of the increased demands on teacher time made by pupils with special needs, some schools were able to appoint additional staff. These could be used to provide support for individual pupils, either in class or on a withdrawal basis. Sometimes the additional staff were not directly concerned with pupils with special needs but were deployed within the school so as to reduce class size and increase flexibility within the timetable.

3. *Recruiting a specialist teacher*

Schools catering for a larger number of pupils with special needs, whether based on mainstream classes or in a unit, found it advantageous to have teachers with an appropriate background in special education on the staff. These teachers were able to coordinate the education of pupils with special needs and act as reference persons to whom staff could go for help and advice. Such teachers, here referred to as 'designated teachers', may be appointed from the special education sector or from the mainstream.

The variety of skills and responsibilities associated with this post are detailed below. Because of these wide-ranging demands, several considerations must be borne in mind when establishing and making appointments to such posts. First, the designated teacher should have proven classroom experience. This was often more important to mainstream staff than qualifications or prior experience in special education. If the designated teacher was perceived to be a skilled practitioner, other staff were more likely to solicit and act on his/her advice.

Second, the wide-ranging responsibilities involved in the role must be reflected in the status of the post. The appointment should be made at a sufficiently high level to ensure that decisions can be made and implemented with a minimum of delay. Finally, the extent of the post's responsibilities must be clearly defined from the outset to avoid misunderstandings on the part of other staff. For example, it should be made clear whether or not disruptive pupils and pupils with mild learning difficulties are included. These pupils are often perceived by mainstream staff as having special educational needs, and there are accordingly expectations that the designated teacher will be expert on their needs.

4. *Ancillary staff*

Teachers identified ancillary staff as a valuable resource for any integration programme. They could provide a level of support that freed teachers to concentrate on teaching by reducing demands of a non-teaching nature. The number of ancillary staff made available to schools varied considerably, reflecting LEA and school policy. Some schools had to manage without any additional ancillary staff under circumstances in which other schools had been allocatd additional staff.

Ancillary staff in the schools studied came from a variety of backgrounds and engaged in a wide range of tasks. Some schools required ancillary staff to have qualified status such as NNEB, SRB or SEN. Others dispensed with formal qualifications but looked for various personal qualities such as flexibility and a high degree of interpersonal skills. Since many mainstream teachers, particularly at secondary level, were unused to working with another adult present, it was important that the ancillary be someone they could relate to easily.

Role of the designated teacher

The role of the designated teacher was typically multi-faceted. Not every component of the role was present in every case, but invariably it called for skill in relating effectively to pupils, other staff and outside agencies. The various facets of the role identified in practice are outlined below.

i) *Teaching pupils with special educational needs*

This task was the predominant one for most designated teachers, taking up at least 50 per cent of allocated teaching time. In the majority of schools, a large proportion of such teaching was conducted by withdrawing pupils individually. At primary level withdrawal gave opportunity for instruction in basic subjects while simultaneously monitoring reading skills and general progress. At secondary level the main focus of withdrawal teaching was on back-up support. It was stressed by several staff that a balance had to be sought between special help and mainstream teaching, since too much extraction could result in a pupil's failing to participate fully in the school curriculum. Both subject and specialist teachers in the secondary sector favoured withdrawal from the whole of one subject rather than from one or two lessons here and there. They felt that the pupil was made to feel different from peers by missing part of one subject, and was faced with the additional problem of catching up on missed work when returning to the mainstream in such a situation.

ii) *Monitoring progress of pupils with special needs*

The designated teacher was generally responsible for keeping records on individual pupils. This teacher also tended to carry out initial assessments when pupils with special needs arrived at the school. Increasingly, schools were endeavouring to build up comprehensive, systematic profiles of individual pupils. At primary level such profiles included infant checklists as well as reading and maths records which indicated what work had been covered and what the pupil had practised and understood. At secondary level it was usual for assessment and progress sheets to be compiled on a six-monthly basis.

Such profiles were considered necessary to cover for staff absences or changes and to provide information at case conferences. The latter, when convened, tended to take up considerable teacher time but were regarded as an opportunity for the various agencies concerned with the pupil to come together to assess progress and discuss future needs. Case conferences tended to be held prior to a school change or to the choice of examination subjects.

iii) *Devising pupil programmes*

Once an initial assessment had been carried out, staff were in a position to know the strengths and weaknesses of the pupil. Such information was used by the designated teacher to decide on a programme of work for that pupil.

Programmes devised for pupils with special needs were typically built around the strengths rather than the weaknesses of the pupils concerned. Care was taken to ensure that pupils experienced success, and subjects from the mainstream time-table were only gradually included in the programme as staff became convinced of the pupil's ability to cope. Sometimes designated teachers remarked that they felt they were being a little over cautious, but defended this on the grounds that pupils needed time to adjust to the pace of mainstream education.

Designated teachers remarked on the usefulness of attending currciulum meetings in all subject areas to ensure adequate knowledge of the curriculum offered and awareness of areas likely to present difficulty, so that they could properly devise programmes according to pupil needs. There were many instances reported in which mainstream staff consulted with the designated teacher over the suitability of mainstream class work for the pupil with special needs.

iv)   *Supporting the mainstream teacher*

The *modus operandi* for supporting mainstream staff followed a two-pronged approach, with designated staff working within classrooms alongside mainstream staff and outside the class on a variety of tasks associated with the pupils' programmes.

a)   Supporting mainstream staff within the classroom
In-class support by a teacher in charge was relatively rare since it was perceived to be expensive in terms of teacher time. (Details are given in chapter 13.) In those schools where such arrangements were made it was considered a very valuable strategy, as it enabled mainstream staff to proceed at a normal pace without having to attend to the work of the pupil with special needs. Being in the mainstream group enabled the designated teacher to gauge where help was most needed and how it might be mediated to individual pupils and provided a useful basis around which informal discussions on individual pupils could be conducted.

b)   Supporting mainstream staff outside the classroom
The primary focus of this task was to provide back up for the

work of the class teacher. It involved the designated teacher in carrying out appropriate preparatory or follow-up work for pupil or class teacher, preparing appropriate materials and discussing teaching approaches with subject teachers.

Various tactics were used for this support work. At one secondary school educating visually handicapped pupils the teacher in charge provided the support in the context of a resource base. This base was organized along very practical lines and was utilized for a variety of purposes. It housed a store of braille books and was used by pupils operating the closed circuit television equipment. Teachers were encouraged to use the available space as a teaching and library area, while specialist staff carried out most of the transcribing work there. The teacher in charge of the visually handicapped provided advice and guidance on teaching methods and materials for subject staff, none of whom had any special training for this kind of work.

At another school educating hearing impaired pupils the designated teacher met weekly with mainstream subject staff to discuss lesson plans. This enabled the former to have advance briefing on the content of lessons so that material could be reviewed with pupils prior to lessons. Introducing pupils to new concepts and vocabulary in advance helped them toward a better understanding of class material as it was presented. Other schools based the support work on half-termly plans discussed at department meetings which the designated teacher also attended. By knowing lesson content in advance, the designated teacher was able to acquire appropriate materials or translate content into an appropriate mode, braille, for example, or on to tape. In some cases the teacher in charge rephrased the language used for school examinations according to pupils' needs.

At primary level support work focused on ensuring that the pupil was adequately versed in basic subjects. For hearing impaired pupils language work was given priority. By secondary level the focus of support had changed with a greater emphasis being placed on lesson content; as it was impossible to cover all lessons satisfactorily essential features were picked out to ensure that pupils understood key concepts.

v)   *Teaching mainstream classes*

In several schools visited it was policy for the designated teacher
to be timetabled to teach some mainstream groups since it was
considered important that the teacher in charge of special needs
was perceived to be an effective member of ordinary teaching
staff. The time available for such teaching, particularly if the staff
member was unit-based, was of necessity very little, but
nevertheless gave specialist staff the opportunity to teach
mainstream groups and maintain familiarity with mainstream
settings.

In other schools the designated teacher provided a reciprocal
service for some mainstream pupils who experienced difficulty
in particular areas. This was exemplified in one primary school
educating pupils with physical handicaps from a unit base. The
teacher in charge would withdraw mainstream pupils into the
unit while unit pupils were in the mainstream. Alternatively a
designated teacher might take a smaller group of pupils within a
mainstream class alongside the class teacher. It was considered
important that both teachers and pupils should integrate in the
teaching and learning processes of the school.

vi)   *Disseminating information*

The mainstream teacher is concerned with acquiring knowledge
about a pupil with special needs sufficient to understand the
nature of any handicapping conditions and how they may
influence that pupil's learning. Responsibility for passing on
such information usually fell to the teacher in charge of pupils
with special needs. The various means used to disseminate
information are discussed in the next chapter. They were usually
influenced by the organizational structure of the school. The
amount of information, however, was generally left to the
discretion of the designated teacher and any detailed information was given to staff concerned directly. The designated
teacher was also responsible for alerting staff to any changes in a

pupil's condition which might affect the pupil's ability to learn efficiently within a mainstream setting.

vii) *Promoting staff development*

Mainstream staff need to acquire sufficient expertise to manage pupils with special needs within an ordinary classroom. Such knowledge may be acquired by association in school with a specialist or designated teacher or through some form of in-service training as discussed in chapter 9. Designated teachers at some schools were responsible for organizing in-service courses for colleagues. When this happened it was usually the result of an initiative taken by designated teachers themselves, who felt that colleagues would benefit from this training input.

viii) *Administration*

Many designated teachers remarked on the inordinate amount of time spent on administrative work, usually without any time-table allocation for it. Contact has to be maintained with a large number of professionals, and a great deal of time was taken up with routine correspondence, arranging visits outside school, maintaining records and receiving visitors. Specialist equipment had to be checked and maintained in good working order. Some staff had to oversee transport arrangements, check hospital appointments and administer drugs. Instances were reported where designated teachers spent time visiting pupils in hospital, checking and ensuring work was available for them and negotiating for the resources needed in mainstream classes.

A further administrative task was organizing the timetable for pupils with special needs. Because of the flexible arrangements made for these pupils this could be a complex task, as discussed in chapter 4. It had to be fitted in after the main school timetable was arranged. In addition, consideration had to be given to the structure and ethos of the receiving class, to the personality of teacher and pupil concerned and to the deployment of extra teacher or ancillary time.

ix)   *Liaising with external agencies*

Many designated teachers saw themselves as a buffer between external agencies and mainstream staff and these contacts could take a great deal of time. Much of the work involved liaising with educational psychologists, social workers, physiotherapists and careers services, to formulate programmes of work or future placements and jobs. Many such contacts were along informal lines but gave an opportunity to discuss general isues. On other occasions the setting was quite formal as in case conferences. The major difficulty for many staff was arranging their time to be free for such meetings without losing too much teaching time. Again, many staff remarked that their timetable did not allow for the large amounts of time such work took.

Deployment of ancillaries

In most schools ancillaries were initially employed as helpers with emphasis on the care of the pupil. Many pupils with special needs benefit from a degree of caring support. Physically handicapped pupils especially may require considerable help in getting around the school or with toileting. Other pupils with severe learning or sensory impairments may need constant supervision while in a mainstream classroom. Medication has to be provided regularly for some pupils. Ancillaries were generally responsible for equipment such as wheelchairs and walkers and ensured they were available when required by pupils. Checking the arrival and departure of pupils was another daily task.

In addition to their care role, ancillaries made a considerable contribution to their pupils' education in some schools. This is discussed and exemplified in chapter 13; suffice it here to note that ancillaries constitute a major staffing resource whose imaginative deployment can greatly enhance the education of pupils with special needs in mainstream settings.

A third way in which ancillaries were used was to engage in

general duties such as recording TV/radio programmes, preparing worksheets for the class and marking books or tests. The intention was that such tasks occupied time when the ancillaries were not required by the pupils, but there was an occasional tendency for ancillaries' time to be completely taken up with general tasks to a point where they took precedence over support of a more specific nature. At one middle school several staff were worried that pupils were unable to take part fully in some lessons such as PE or science because ancillary staff were unavailable, being busy with general tasks. One secondary school used ancillary staff primarily for administration work, reluctantly releasing them for support in specific areas.

The organization and deployment of ancillary support raised problems in some schools, particularly when there were several ancillaries employed in the school. Ideally, they were at the disposition of the teacher in charge of special needs who deployed them in the most efficient way bearing the needs of individual pupils in mind. In some schools, however, ancillary staff operated quite independently of the teaching staff, deciding themselves what tasks they would carry out and even drawing up their own timetables. In other schools their work and deployment were decided by the head without reference to teaching staff. In one secondary school the four welfare assistants were under the authority of the matron; their use remained outside the jurisdiction of the teacher in charge of special needs and, in fact, they engaged mainly in clerical duties. Several teachers were dissatisfied at what they saw as misuse of ancillary support.

In all cases observed where the ancillaries acted separately and independently of mainstream staff, the ancillaries had access to information about individual pupils and one task was to disseminate this information as requested by teachers. The latter resented having to go to ancillary staff in this way, feeling that as professional staff they should have priority access to information on individual pupils.

Much of this resentment could be dissipated by having more open procedures for deciding the workload of ancillaries. It was noticeable that in schools where the use of ancillary staff was democratically decided their time was organized to ensure it was for the optimum benefit of staff and pupils alike. The deployment of ancillaries in these situations was decided by teacher discussion at staff meetings and by mutual agreement between teacher and ancillary. Classroom support, particularly in practical lessons, was given priority ensuring the best use of teacher time and full participation of pupils with special needs in lessons.

Liaison

The presence of pupils with special needs in a school increases the need for liaison both within the school and between school staff and external agencies. The latter can include psychologists, speech therapists, physiotherapists, doctors, social workers, advisory and peripatetic teaching staff. All these external agencies can have an influence on the education of pupils with special needs, and there is need of co-operative work with teachers. It is expected that the implementation of the 1981 Act will further this co-operation between teachers and other professionals. How schools have coped with the problem of liaison among staff and between staff and other professionals is discussed here.

a)   *Liaison between staff*

The staffing changes outlined above point to the need for clear lines of communication. These may be based on a previous system in the school or entail a new and radical approach, but in either case require a single person to have overall responsibility for coordinating and disseminating information about individual pupils. Such a role may fall to an already established teacher within the remedial department or be part of the duties of the specialist or designated teacher.

There is also a need to monitor pupils' programmes and to ensure that any work done outside mainstream classes is related to the work within the mainstream group. Several schools have organized 'written records' procedures which are then collated. These entailed gathering information about any pupils causing concern. Written comments from staff revealed areas where a pupil may have needed extra help, and acted as a record of progress. Similar written records were kept to monitor progress in subject areas and to ensure a balanced 'diet' for the pupil concerned. One secondary school devised written record sheets for these purposes. One sheet (example 1) was used in the unit base to record the work done in the unit when mainstream teachers took the class. The other sheet (example 2) was used by staff to record the work covered and progress made by pupils when in mainstream classes. The use of these sheets made it possible to identify and deal with any difficulties quickly.

EXAMPLE 1
Staff-based record

Week ending . . . .

To be used when mainstream staff are taking pupils in the unit

	1	2	3	4	5
Monday					
Tuesday					
Wednesday					
Thursday					
Friday					

The transfer and recording of information between staff is time-consuming and requires a flexibility in the timetable to allow staff to meet. This is particularly important for co-ordinating staff, who need to be able to talk to mainstream staff when they are free. This flexibility has to be built into staff timetables and allowed for when considering the staffing needs of a school.

EXAMPLE 2
Report-base record

Name _____ Class _____ Tutor _____

To be filled in by staff

W/ending	Day	Work covered	Comments/progress etc.	Staff

Review/recommendation

Signature . . . .

b) *Liaison between staff and outside agencies*

Mainstream staff reported contact with a variety of external agencies but such contact was often irregular and unsatisfactory. The problem seemed to lie in the dichotomy of perception about the role of external agencies as between the teachers and the agencies themselves. Many of the agencies saw their main role as supporting pupils directly whereas teachers sought to use the agencies as sources of information, guidance and resources.

Several schools having pupils supported by peripatetic staff found difficulty in arranging for peripatic staff to have meetings with class teachers. Because of heavy workloads peripatetic staff had only limited time in a school, and this did not allow for teacher discussion. Teachers were often disappointed with the advice and support available from the LEA advisory service. Educational psychologists could be a major resource for teachers, being in a position not only to know in detail a pupil's strengths and weaknesses but able to draw up a suitable programme of work. Here again staffing limitations allied to large assessment caseloads meant that teachers were often disappointed and received little of practical benefit in the classroom.

A considerable number of schools were receiving help from speech therapists and physiotherapists. In most cases these professionals visited on a regular basis but the efficacy of their work was dependent on the availability of staff in school to continue the programmes on a daily basis. It was not usually possible for a mainstream teacher to cope with such additional demands and this work fell to ancillaries when available. Mainstream staff had very little direct contact with these services and, perhaps in consequence, often perceived them as being relatively unimportant. Such therapy as was available tended to be carried out in lunchtimes or breaks as mainstream staff were generally against losing teaching time to therapy of any kind. If withdrawal from class was necessary, close cooperation was required so that the teacher could tailor activities around known appointments.

There will inevitably be organizational problems in bringing together a varied group of professionals, and one result may well be increased demands on teacher time. The appointment of a designated teacher can be a key factor in containing these demands. As discussed above, designated teachers can play a major facilitating role in linking between staff within the school and between school staff and external agencies.

Chapter 8
Information

The acquisition of relevant information about pupils with special needs was a major issue with the mainstream teachers interviewed. They had no wish to become instant experts on special needs but did desire to know more about the pupils they taught. In particular, they wanted information about their capabilities and limitations and about any other matters which had implications for teaching them. Many teachers expressed disquiet at the lack of such information or at the difficulty in obtaining it.

In this chapter, we look at the variety of ways in which schools organized the transmission of information to teachers. Many schools were still exploring how to set about doing this, and indeed were asking what should be regarded as necessary or appropriate information. This being so, it was not surprising to find that mainstream staff in the majority of schools studied were relatively uninformed about pupils with special needs in their schools.

It should be recalled that most of the research was carried out prior to the implementation of the 1981 Education Act, and it is expected that implementation will lead to improvement in this area. The Act requires that the governors or the LEA, as appropriate, ensure that all a pupil's special educational needs 'are made known to all who are likely to teach him'. Circular 1/83 elaborates on these duties. It also recognized the key position that the class teacher holds. The teacher 'is in the best position to recognize when a pupil is experiencing difficulties and to try out different approaches to help meet these needs'. It is expected too that professionals involved with the assessment of pupils with special needs will work closely with class teachers and that information from professional consultations and assessments will be kept on file alongside teacher records of their pupils' progress.

Schools in our study used a variety of means to transmit information: compiling and distributing lists; giving access to pupil files; using staff meetings and direct personal contact.

1. Lists

The basic reason for compiling lists of pupils with special needs was to notify staff of their presence in the school. This was a common procedure, with the list of names being given out to each teacher or pinned to a noticeboard. Such lists served the function of announcing their presence without drawing undue attention to it, though of course the mere fact of compiling a list necessarily singled out pupils to some extent.

Many head teachers favoured the use of a simple list of names – without any additional information – and pointed to several advantages. Apart from helping to keep the presence of pupils with special needs unobtrusive, it saved staff from becoming overloaded with information and guarded against negative reaction and preconceived ideas about pupils before they arrived in class. On the other hand, the lack of background information is a drawback if the result is that teachers are unaware of the impact a handicapping condition can have on pupils' learning. This was exemplified in one secondary school which had a unit catering for pupils with specific learning difficulties. Many staff had a very limited understanding of the kinds of difficulties experienced by these pupils and were quite unfamiliar with the teaching strategies appropriate to them. As a consequence, they tended to regard them simply as having low ability and saw no need for contact with unit staff.

Lists were sometimes extended, usually with details of reading age and handicapping condition, possibly with reference to how this might affect the pupil's educational development. One secondary school with a unit for hearing impaired pupils issued each member of staff with detailed notes on individual pupils, focusing on the impact the impairment would have on their learning. These notes drew attention to the difficulties that

pupils might experience in mainstream classes and suggested
techniques for staff to use which would help pupils to participate
fully in a mainstream setting.

An intermediate approach was to furnish staff with a list of
names and leave it to them to supplement it with specific
information as required. This could be done by reference to
individual pupils' files or by consulting specialist staff. This had
the benefit of giving staff the information that they needed to
know – and no more – and entrusting them with the responsibility of acquiring it. On the negative side, such a policy could
be hit-and-miss. There was no guarantee that information was
communicated effectively, or even accurately. Moreover, it
would be unwise to assume that staff who perceive no need for
additional information are in fact adequately informed!

2.   Pupil files

Pupils usually atttended their individual schools over a number
of years, during which time information about them was collated
and put on file. For reasons of confidentiality access to such files
was often limited to very few staff, although selected information
was made available to staff generally if deemed necesary.

A few schools, which issued lists of pupils with special needs,
gave access to further information through the pupil files to staff
who wanted more information. Although access to the files gave
mainstream staff the opportunity to see all the information on
the pupils concerned, it had several disadvantages. First, the
contents of the files might not be directly relevant to teaching
the pupils concerned, so that teachers needed guidance in
extracting and interpreting information from them. Second, the
onus was placed on the mainstream teacher to seek out this
information, and many staff who would have benefited from
further information did not, because of lack of time or
inclination. Third, a great deal of time could be wasted in
tracking down a keyholder to unlock doors or cabinets to
relevant files.

The problem of confidentiality regarding the release of
information on pupils should arise less as progress is made on
the implementation of the 1981 Education Act, since written
information is to be confined to a pupil's special needs and how

they are to be met. Any other details which may give rise to problems of confidentiality or professional ethics need not be included. Also, the problem of irrelevant information should be diminished since Circular 1/83 stipulates that 'Professional advice should be relevant and usable in an educational context'. Although Circular 1/83 considers the implications of the 1981 Education Act and offers advice to LEAs on the formulating and receiving of statements for some pupils with special needs, it is recognized that relatively few pupils will require the protection of a statement. The Act however does place an obligation on LEAs to ensure that adequate provision is made for all pupils with special educational needs. It is to be hoped therefore that some of the practices enjoined in the statementing procedure will be followed for pupils with special educational needs not requiring a statement.

3. Staff meetings

Some schools gave priority to ensuring that staff gained information about pupils with special needs directly, and specific times were set aside when all staff could be brought together to discuss such pupils. These meetings gave opportunity for staff to ask questions, obtain information specific to their own teaching and raise matters of concern. Teachers at schools which used staff meetings to relay information frequently remarked that these meetings should be held separately from normal staff meetings in order to give adequate time for discussion and questioning. Such meetings could be expensive in terms of staff time, but they were conducive to a comprehensive exchange of information and helped mainstream staff to relate the available information to their teaching practice.

At one primary school which contained a large number of pupils with a variety of handicapping conditions, weekly sessions were held to discuss all pupils with special needs. All staff attended these meetings, including ancillary staff. Points were raised about individual progress and any problems arising within the mainstream setting. There was a free exchange of information and ideas, with staff able to draw on each other's experience. In addition, before any pupil with special needs was placed in a mainstream lesson there was a formal group meeting comprising head, deputy head, specialist teacher and class teacher receiving the pupil. These meetings ensured that necessary information about the pupil was passed directly to the receiving teacher together with advice on appropriate teaching approaches and materials.

Such frequent staff meetings were not always judged necessary. Several schools arranged meetings at monthly intervals, at which staff could identify pupils they were concerned about and pool ideas on programmes and teaching approaches. One large secondary school catering for pupils with a diversity of special needs found it easier to arrange staff discussions around year group meetings, which occurred twice a term. It was felt that a meeting with a smaller number of staff who were directly concerned with pupils led to more focused discussion and ensured that information was transmitted more effectively.

4. Peripatetic staff
Teachers in a large number of schools depended on peripatetic staff for detailed information on pupils with special needs and for advice on appropriate teaching techniques. Such staff possessed the advantage of knowing about and having access to the resources that mainstream teachers or individual pupils might require. Apart from their own expertise, peripatetic staff were also frequently in a position to advise and give information about practice in other schools facing similar situations.

The major weakness of this approach is that peripatetic staff are generally not on site daily nor for long periods. In many instances this was a source of disquiet among staff, who because of timetabling or other constraints had difficulty in getting to see the peripatetic teacher. In one school staff resorted to using a system of notes to and from the peripatetic teacher since direct contact was rarely possible. Apart from being indirect, this was sometimes inefficient and slow. One head of a small secondary school, which was totally dependent on peripatetic teachers for specialist information, did arrange for the latter to attend staff meetings on the days they visited the school. Mainstream staff found this arrangement very helpful and were reassured by the knowledge that regular contact could be made if necessary. Another secondary school, catering for a large number of partially hearing pupils supported by peripatetic help, was able to arrange for the peripatetic teacher to spend a whole day in the school approximately once a month. During this time staff could arrange to see the specialist teacher.

5. Designated teacher

The transmission of information was greatly enhanced by the presence in a school of a teacher responsible for pupils with special needs. Such a teacher acted as a source and coordinator of information about pupils as well as being a link person between mainstream staff and outside agencies. Several schools in our study catering for a variety of pupils with special needs were visited by advisory and peripatetic staff, who provided pupil support but had few dealings with mainstream staff. As a result school staff were missing out on information and curricular advice that could have been made available. In the absence of a teacher with responsibility for pupils with special needs, there was no ready means of extracting this information and advice from visiting staff or of collating it for the benefit of school staff. By contrast, in those schools where there was a designated teacher, staff were more likely to be informed about the problems of individual pupils and to know where advice could be sought.

The appointment of a teacher in charge of pupils with special needs at one middle school demonstrates the value of such a post for the transmission of information. The school has on roll a number of pupils with either severe visual or physical impairments, and encountered a number of difficulties because no one on the staff had specific responsibility for special needs. In particular, it took a long time to acquire specialist resources, and specific information about pupils did not always reach staff. The peripatetic teacher for the visually impaired pupils who visited the school each week saw pupils but did not have time for discussion with class teachers. The latter found this unsatisfactory as they wanted a better understanding of the nature of the handicaps and how to meet pupils' needs. Because of the lack of information many staff felt anxious and even resentful of the presence of these pupils in large mixed ability classes. Some of these problems were resolved by the appointment of a teacher in charge of special needs. This teacher, working a flexible timetable, acted as a link person with the peripatetic teacher, relayed advice and materials to mainstream staff and arranged for a short in-service morning on visual impairment. Mainstream staff also saw her as a source of information on individual pupils.

In summary, it is to be hoped that the impetus given to recording information on pupils by the 1981 Education Act and the associated statementing procedures will encourage schools to review the ways in which staff acquire information, whether it be basic details on pupils' handicapping conditions, information on resources or guidance on teaching approaches. The procedures used in many schools are far from efficient. (The potentially valuable resource of peripatetic staff in particular is poorly used.) This state of affairs can hardly be allowed to continue; teachers need ready and comprehensive access to the best available information if they are to deploy their professional skills to best advantage in devising and implementing individual programmes of work for pupils with special needs.

Chapter 9
School Based In-service Training

The Warnock Report recognized the fact that ordinary teachers would require further training if they were to provide an adequate education for pupils with special needs in mainstream. It was envisaged that in-service training would be made available on three levels:

a) Short courses for all teachers concerned with special needs
b) One year full-time courses or part-time equivalents
c) A range of advanced short courses.

Such courses were to provide mainstream staff with sufficient knowledge of special educational needs and background information to give an understanding of these needs and the implications for teaching. It was also recognized that certain skills would be needed if the teacher was to recognize and secure help for such pupils and was to adopt the most appropriate teaching strategies. This knowledge and the skills acquired through training would help secure positive attitudes toward pupils with special needs in mainstream.

To provide such a comprehensive range of courses would necessitate local, regional and national planning together with considerable financial input. This has not been forthcoming on anything like the scale required. Many mainstream teachers reported that they had been unable to attend any course relating to pupils with special needs and saw little prospect of attending suitable courses in the near future. This is not to say that there has not been an increase in the number of courses available but there is still an urgent need to extend the range of courses available.

This chapter is concerned with school-based in-service

training already available in different areas of the country, which has enabled teachers to work more successfully with pupils having special educational needs. Such training has not involved LEAs in a heavy financial investment, and was achieved by local school-based courses and by mainstream teachers having professional contact with colleagues from special education.

School-based courses

The team found that many schools were organizing their own in-service training for staff rather than waiting for the LEA to do so. Indeed, much of this school-based in-service training arose from internal discussion about staff needs and development. School-based in-service training courses presented themselves as an efficient and low cost method of promoting staff development.

Each course studied by the team was said to need a pre-planning stage to focus attention on constraints and identify key problem areas before the course started. Another essential feature was an in-built evaluation factor which allowed enough flexibility for the course to meet the changing needs of teachers. Evaluation was done informally on the basis of staff room discussion for the most part. The courses were reported to have been catalysts for changes in schools, as well as promoting relevant staff development.

Most school-based in-service activities were found to take place out of school hours with little or no release of teaching staff. To encourage as many staff to attend as possible, several tactics were found to be useful in removing obstacles that might otherwise deter staff. Dates of meetings were carefully chosen to avoid times when staff were heavily committed, e.g. examination periods. These dates were published as early as possible and conspicuously displayed. Every member of staff was kept informed of the in-service programme, and if members of staff did not attend a meeting it was never assumed they were not interested. Follow-up discussions revealed other possible staff requirements and these needs could be met during the course. Such activities maintained the goodwill of staff, already hard pressed but giving up free time to attend these courses, and increased the effectiveness of the courses.

Two examples of courses are given below. Both demonstrate the scope and feasibility of tapping the expertise available in the special education sector. The two examples given by no means exhaust the organizational possibilities, and the team came across many other instances in which mainstream schools used local special school staff for in-service training purposes.

The first example was organized by the staff of a mainstream primary school having on roll a large number of pupils with a variety of special educational needs. The course took place before the pupils with special needs arrived at the school and was attended by all staff. It has not been repeated since no new staff have been employed at the school. Moreover, specialist staff are available on site to advise and help mainstream teachers so the need for specific in-service training has been reduced. The course was organized jointly by the staff who, having decided what their needs were, approached the education authority and nearby special schools in order to tap all available expertise. The aims and structure of the course were clearly laid out, and the effort was made to relate the content closely to the specific situation of that school. Many of the staff remarked on the value of visiting special schools for a whole day as well as having speakers on particular disabilities. The course required staff to give up a good deal of time for meetings after school and for residential weekends but it was regarded as extremely valuable in helping mainstream staff to manage pupils with a variety of special needs.

EXAMPLE I: School in-service induction course

1. *Aims*

To induct mainstream primary school staff (teaching and ancillary workers) into the philosophy, organization and methodology of special education.

To induct staff from a special education background into

the philosophy, organization and methodology of mainstream primary education.

To provide space for staff with widely differing backgrounds to gel together and become an integrated school staff.

To examine current trends, the national scene and the Warnock Report in the context of the school.

To discuss integration, organization and curriculum in the light of future developments at the school.

To produce guidelines for the integration of children with special needs and mainstream primary school children.

2. Course structure

Three elements:
A Weekly staff meetings to which specialist speakers were invited
B Visits to establishments catering for children with special needs
C A residential element of one weekend's duration
Elements A and B were concurrent.
Element C followed at the end of the course.

ELEMENT A: STAFF MEETINGS (TOTAL 11 MEETINGS)
These were designed to impart information, establish dialogue and stimulate further thinking and reading. The format included visiting speakers followed by small group discussions and staff workshops

To introduce the course an overview was presented by an LEA adviser and included in a report on the national scene, special education provision in the locality and the role expected of the school. The Warnock Report formed the basis for the rest of the element.

The school has on roll four categories of children having special needs: broadly speaking, those who previously would have been categorized as ESN(M) (Educationally Sub Normal (Moderate)), partially hearing, visually impaired and maladjusted. Two meetings were held to examine each category.

The first was led by a visiting speaker who outlined the problems of the group and the possibilities for integration into mainstream primary education. This provided the basis for discussion and further consideration at the second meeting which consisted of small group discussions or workshops.

ELEMENT B: VISITS TO OTHER EDUCATIONAL ESTABLISHMENTS
Staff were able to spend at least two whole days visiting special schools and units where they could observe and converse with other teachers. Opportunities were made available to them to teach for part of the day in the school visited. The help of the LEA advisory service was obtained in selecting and coordinating suitable visits. The first session of Element B was given over to staff discussion of the purpose of the visits and to detailed planning of how to carry them out. Two reporting sessions were held after the visits to pass information on to colleagues and discuss impressions formed. The first of these took place after the first phase of visits and the second on conclusion of visits.

TIMETABLE

All meetings to be held on Wednesdays from 3.30pm to finish not later than 5.00pm.

	ELEMENT A	ELEMENT B
Session 1		Planning of visits, format, recording
Session 2	Adviser. An overview	
Session 3	Adviser. Role of the school Admission and assessment procedures	

Session 4 Education of hearing
              impaired children

Session 5 Private session: staff
              review

H A L F   T E R M

Session 6 Open forum

Session 7   Private session: review
                                   of visits

Session 8 Education of ESN(M)

Session 9 Private session: staff
              review

Session 10 Education of maladjusted
              children

Session 11 Private session: staff
              review

E A S T E R

Session 12   Final review of all visits

Session 13 Education of visually
              handicapped

Session 14 Private session: staff
              review

ELEMENT C
This was organized as a residential weekend for all staff at the
conclusion of the course. The cost was borne by the LEA. The
weekend included a mixture of workshop/discussion groups
whose task was to produce guidelines for integration within

the school and workshop/discussions with LEA advisers and special speakers from the course.

The second example is a course run for mainstream staff in a secondary school who have partially hearing pupils in their classes. It is compulsory for all probationary teachers at the school. The course is organized on site by staff from the attached partial hearing unit. It lasts between eight and ten weeks, at the end of which the teachers are given a certificate of completion by the authority. The major part of the course is arranged after school, but visits to special schools take place during school time. Teachers found the course useful in alerting them to the needs of partially hearing pupils and in giving them confidence to manage these pupils in the mainstream. The content of the course is outlined in the following extracts from school documents.

EXAMPLE II: In-service Training
(as proposed by a Mainstream High School and attached Partial Hearing Unit)

This is a scheme directed initially at probationary teachers on the permanent staff roll. It is also recommended that it should be a compulsory training scheme. It is also available to any members of staff joining the school; particularly welcome are established teachers who have had no prior experience of pupils with hearing impairments.

Aim

It is intended to inform teachers and extend their general understanding, acquired during their training for the Certificate of Education, of the handicapped pupil, within the context of the Warnock Report.

Schemes

Schemes of work to include:
1. understanding types of deafness
2. causes of deafness
   interpreting an audiogram
   use of an audiometer . . . ordinary hearing/those with hearing impairments
3. the effect different hearing losses have on achieving speech . . . social problems which can arise from hearing impairment
4. positioning of hearing impaired pupil in class . . . reasons for this . . . practical demonstrations . . . lighting . . . boards, etc.
5. identifying whether the hearing impaired pupil has really understood . . . practical dictation work . . . common mistakes in lipreading . . . mistakes caused by their deafness
6. sign language and its role . . . first language of the hearing impaired . . . importance of facial expressions . . . understanding those with speech defects as a result of hearing problems
7. manner in which to treat hearing impaired pupils . . expectancy in academic/social development
8. practical teaching of a hearing impaired pupil on subject of one's choice . . . retention span . . . whether they can communicate a specific fact . . . how they will incorporate the hearing impaired as a member of their form/class.

This course is intended to be practical rather than theoretical. The technical equipment used by teachers of the deaf and the hearing aids in general will be demonstrated throughout the course, or when it is necessary to do so. Visits e.g. to a school for the deaf and a partial hearing clinic will occur when convenient to both parties. The course is supplemented by in-class help from unit staff and literature produced in the unit.

Professional contacts

Those staff with a special education background are in a position to share knowledge and expertise with their mainstream colleagues. Such staff include on-site specialists, peripatetic staff, visiting educational psychologists and advisers. Mainstream staff can further their professional development by association with these colleagues from special education. The advantage of this kind of in-service training is that it is practically based and is related to the immediate environment. A corresponding drawback is that knowledge acquired in this way can be patchy and lacking in coherence.

The main constraint on building up this form of professional contact is shortage of time. Schools employed a variety of tactics to make professional expertise available to mainstream staff on a more regular basis. Such tactics included making time available during the school day for informal contacts and timetabling specialist staff in mainstream to work alongside or as part of a team with mainstream colleagues. Some schools persuaded staff with a special education background to provide semi-formal courses for their mainstream colleagues.

Many schools educating pupils with sensory impairment favoured a team teaching approach so that specialist teachers worked alongside mainstream staff. The latter were thus able to learn by watching expert colleagues working with these pupils. In a small Midlands primary school which planned to admit hearing impaired pupils, two specialist teachers were appointed one term before the first pupils arrived. During this period they worked as ordinary teachers, at the same time building up resources and providing in-service training for all staff in preparation for the arrival of the hearing impaired pupils. Certainly the ethos of the open plan school plus the integrated day had resulted in teachers being particularly flexible and ready to accept a new challenge, but the way in which the preparations were made gave the programme an excellent start. Both specialist staff continued to teach in mainstream mixed ability groups, where they felt it was helpful to teachers to see how a teacher of the deaf talked to hearing impaired pupils and in particular how vocabulary could be explained – techniques best learnt by example.

One secondary school catering for pupils with visual, hearing and learning impairments had been able to appoint a specialist teacher for hearing impaired and a specialist teacher for visually impaired pupils, each on a half-time basis. Mainstream staff had direct access to the specialist teachers; indeed the flexible timetable of the hearing impairment specialist enabled each mainstream teacher to have a meeting with the specialist. The specialist staff saw their role as ensuring that the mainstream teacher received relevant information about the pupil, was given guidance on appropriate teaching techniques and had obtained any necessary materials. They themselves would deal with outside agencies and parents, so reducing the demands on mainstream teachers. This policy of direct access to specialist staff was highly successful in ensuring the goodwill of mainstream teachers.

Where a school has a unit for pupils with special needs on site, or has links with a special school, specialist staff act in much the same way as the designated teacher. The specialist staff provide information about pupils and advise on teaching strategies and materials and may be available to teach in the mainstream. At several secondary schools containing units it was policy that staff attend all curriculum meetings and teach in the mainstream. When specialist staff were seen by mainstream colleagues to have specific mainstream commitments this helped the latter to view them as experts who would moreover be able to give realistic advice.

Having a specialist teacher does not always guarantee such easy exchange of information and ideas. In one primary school class teachers had been coping largely on their own with pupils having a range of physical and learning difficulties. The appointment of a full-time specially trained teacher did not prove particularly successful, as mainstream staff were unused to having a specialist about and were reluctant to work with one. Furthermore, this teacher had no mainstream teaching responsibility and her credibility for offering realistic advice was limited.

Another major source of professional contact were the peripatetic sevices. These have been discussed in detail above and it is clear that, despite the practical difficulties of timetabling and arranging meetings, they had a considerable educative dimension. This was usually focused on specific pupils when class teachers acquired from peripatetic staff some understanding of their handicapping conditions and learning needs and developed appropriate teaching and management skills. Occasionally the expertise of the services was tapped for brief in-service training sessions. At one middle school an in-service morning was arranged by the peripatetic service for mainstream staff who were coping with visually impaired pupils in mainstream situations. The peripatetic teacher also arranged for the tutor in charge of pupils with special needs and the head teacher to visit a special school to view available resources. Peripatetic teachers for the hearing impaired in another authority ensured that they regularly visited schools for a whole day. This meant that they were available to staff to answer queries and offer advice. Another peripatetic teacher regularly arranged in-service evenings for mainstream staff and ancillaries.

Educational psychologists could be an invaluable source of information for the teacher, being in a position not only to know in detail a pupil's strengths and weaknesses but also able to draw up a suitable programme of work. However, services were reported to be so understaffed that the psychologists were not able to see all the pupils that schools asked them to see, and generally offered minimal input to mainstream staff. The service was regarded by many teachers as totally inadequate. The main contribution noted from educational psychologists was their involvement in school-based in-service courses.

Mainstream schools having links with special schools found in them a wealth of expertise which could be made available to mainstream staff. The close links that some special schools had with peripatetic services made it possible for such staff to be available to demonstrate and/or monitor teaching and management techniques to mainstream staff. In some cases staff were loaned from the special school to help develop particular areas of expertise in mainstream schools. One secondary school had brought in special school staff to help plan appropriate programmes for pupils with moderate learning difficulties. In this case, specialist staff were able to share expertise and monitor innovative programmes. If the programme did not produce the expected result it was altered and refined until pupils were able to cope in the mainstream groups.

Whether achieved through formal in-service training or through informal contact with colleagues, the professional development of school staff is an essential component of the process of educating pupils with special needs in the mainstream. Educating these pupils calls for curricular skills and a professional orientation that many teachers in ordinary schools do not possess. Encouraging appropriate staff development must then be given high priority. It is a matter of concern that frequently staff development was not encouraged nor even facilitated by matters such as timetable modifications or teaching cover. Even the modest initiatives described in this chapter were far from typical, while opportunities to go on more extended courses of training were comparatively few. Much is made in this book of the fact that teaching pupils with special needs is not totally different from teaching other pupils. It must be recognized however that particular knowledge and skills are required, and that arrangements for appropriate staff development must be made.

Part Four
Teaching

Chapter 10
Classroom Organization

In much the same way as the layout of a school site affects the ease with which pupils can move from one point to another, similarly the organization of facilities within a classroom influences the way in which an individual pupil can participate in class activities and move about the room as required. The following two statements are taken from the Warnock Report: 'Educational efficiency . . . depends in part upon a physical organization of facilities' and 'Before any scheme of integration is introduced its implications in physical terms must be thoroughly studied and appropriate provision made' (Warnock Report, 1978, p.117). It should be remembered that the majority of pupils with special needs are being taught in classrooms which were not especially designed, located in school buildings which in many cases present problems for all pupils and teachers in terms of space, illumination, access and the dimension of teaching areas. The aim in this chapter is to recognize and record the measures taken in ordinary classrooms to accommodate pupils who have a range of special educational needs. Four aspects of classroom organization are considered: the arrangement of furniture; seating and grouping of pupils; acoustics; lighting.

The arrangement of furniture

Furnishings include both built-in fixtures and those items which can be moved about at the teacher's discretion. The former generally consist of cupboards, shelving, the blackboard and other display areas, sinks, power points, benches and study carrels. Laboratories, workshops and home economics rooms also contain much specialist equipment, most of which is built in. The moveable items usually comprise desks, tables and in some cases small mobile equipment such as trolleys and bookshelves. An increasing number of classrooms now have TV monitors, overhead projectors and computer keyboards. A few classrooms, particularly in primary schools and remedial departments in secondary schools, also have a quiet library area, which may be carpeted and supplied with easy chairs.

The teacher has a degree of control over the arrangement of classroom furniture, but is obviously limited by the size and dimensions of the teaching space, the presence of built-in fixtures, the number of pupils in a given group and the nature of the subject(s) taught. In addition, certain pupils have specific requirements in terms of location in the room and access to specific parts of it, which can influence the arrangement of furniture and in some cases result in the presence of certain items of equipment.

It should be remembered that the mere presence in an ordinary classroom of a pupil with special needs is only a small part of that pupil's total educational requirement. In addition to engaging in academic tasks, the pupil must also function as a social member of the teaching group and should be as independent in this situation as possible. The academic framework is essential, but so also are opportunities for social and emotional development and for interaction with other pupils. It is important therefore that the teaching space be arranged so that it not only facilitates learning but also allows for independent mobility and appropriate socializing.

Our research indicated that for pupils in wheelchairs this situation is more readily achieved in large classrooms and in open plan teaching areas. The traditional classroom is often too small to permit any movement once all pupils have taken their places. Questions of furniture and pupil mobility are not restricted to those in wheelchairs, however. Others too require specialist equipment; depending on pupil need, items such as power points for desk lamps, shelves and cupboards for storing braille machines or braille books or 3D teaching aids, special work tables and bookstands may have to be located. In schools where such items are brought into the room for the pupil, space to use them should be found so that the equipment is as unobtrusive as possible and does not constitute a physical barrier separating the pupils with special needs from the rest of the class.

The arrangement of furniture obviously has greatest importance for pupils whose mobility is restricted, i.e. those who have difficulty in walking or who spend most or all of their time in a wheelchair. Furniture should be placed to give ready access to as much of the room as possible. It was noticeable that the greatest problems were posed in classrooms which were used by several staff and a number of different pupil groups each week. (This is of course a common situation in many secondary schools.) The traditional arrangement of desks and tables in rows with narrow aisles between gave little opportunity for the pupil with mobility problems to do other than remain in one place throughout the lesson. In addition, a wheelchair cannot fit under a traditional desk or table and must of necessity block an aisle. One teacher in this situation had reduced the effect on classroom circulation by creating an extra aisle along the wall beside the door and doubling up the lines of single desks to give more space. The pupil's wheelchair was parked in this side aisle where it was unobtrusive and yet still near the door. Headteachers were aware of the space restrictions in many classrooms and tried, as a matter of policy, to restrict the number of pupils in wheelchairs to a maximum of two per teaching group.

In primary schools, where pupils tend to be based in one classroom, the teacher often has more control over the situation. In one infant department the teacher rearranged the furniture to help a pupil in a wheelchair gain access to all parts of the room and turned the event into a learning situation for all of the pupils by discussing the problem with them. These pupils had learned to push their chairs in when they were not using them and remembered not to leave bags, books or toys on the floor between the blocks of tables. The teacher was very positive over the way in which everyone had responded and said that her main job was to keep the blocks of tables in one place, since during the course of the week they could move slightly after repeated straightening-up processes. Where desks and tables were arranged in blocks this did make an easier and more spacious environment in which a wheelchair could manoeuvre.

While arranging desks or tables in a circle or semi-circle may encourage pupils with hearing impairment to contribute more readily to class discussions, this is clearly not a practicable arrangement in a mainstream classroom in view of the numbers of pupils involved. For small group work however seating pupils in a circle or round a block of tables can be useful, as it enables all pupils to see one another and to contribute equally. To be avoided, especially where there are pupils with sensory handicap present, is the practice of seating pupils at blocks of tables – where some are inevitably facing away from the teacher – and then giving a class lesson, as this presents great problems for those whose sight or hearing is impaired.

Some pupils require the use of special equipment and furniture. It should be remembered too that their needs will change as their medical condition alters and as they become older. Periodically, new or different calipers, braces, wheel-chairs, tables and bookrests may be needed, for example; a pupil may require to spend either more or less time standing up or seated during the day; and pupils can literally outgrow certain items of furniture and equipment. This means of course that there should be budgetary provision for replacements. In our visits to schools we observed great variation between LEAs in the supply of special desks, tables and other special equipment and in the ways in which these were serviced, reviewed and replaced at intervals.

Seating and grouping of pupils

While the ideal might be to permit pupils to choose their own seating positions in the classroom, the teacher must ensure that those with special needs are located in the most suitable position for them to maximize their learning and to participate as fully as possible in all activities. To this end, there are certain principles to be borne in mind. The hearing impaired should sit where they can make the most of what is seen and heard in the room and ideally should be located about six to ten feet from the main speaker – usually the teacher – and slightly to one side. Many staff felt that a position in the second row of a traditionally arranged room was about right, and if a pupil were to one side of the room he or she could readily turn to face another pupil who was speaking. It is important that a pupil with impaired hearing can clearly see the faces of speakers and so a seating position with a major light source behind or to the side of pupils is preferable to one which calls for pupils to look toward the speaker and the light source. In the latter situation the speaker could appear a silhouette. Also, where two hearing impaired pupils are present in a class they should not sit one behind the other as this of course prevents one from watching the other speaking.

The many different kinds of visual impairment rquire different responses in terms of lighting and seating position in class. A major requirement is that the pupil should be able and indeed encouraged to use residual sight and be free to move as close to the blackboard/whiteboard/overhead projector as necessary at any time. Most teachers found it more successful to let the pupil decide where to sit in a given classroom, checking that the chosen position gave a clear view of the teacher and did not subject the pupil to undue glare or blackboard shine. The latter is a problem for all pupils in some classrooms but exacerbates the sight problems of visually impaired pupils. Most partially sighted pupils preferred to sit centrally and reasonably near the front of a traditionally arranged classroom where the focus was at the front of the room, while blind pupils tended more often than not to sit at the side of the room or toward the back. The walls gave an easy point of reference and where a welfare assistant was present it was felt that she was less conspicuous at the back of the room.

Additional points concerning pupils with severe visual handicap include the following.
1. Any changes in room layout or arrangement of tables or desks should be followed by an individual re-orientation session, so that these pupils can continue to find their way round the classroom with confidence.
2. Classroom doors should always be fully open or completely shut; half open doors are a hazard.
3. Pupils' bags and briefcases should not be left in the aisles or spaces between desks and tables.

During our visits to schools we noted that the teacher's

sensitivity to the basic needs of visually impaired pupils was quickly picked up by the pupils, who themselves ensured that partially sighted and blind peers were fully involved in classroom activities. For example, we noted that friends provided verbal comments and interpretations, that they read blackboard notes aloud and that they brought visually impaired pupils to the front of informal groups which gathered around the teacher's desk.

Pupils with more severe physical handicaps may require a specific location in the classroom, because of special equipment such as a wheelchair, table, desk or typewriter. Wherever possible, the classroom location should still enable the pupil to communicate with others, since a pupil who has to sit separately or who is permanently accompanied by a welfare assistant can feel quite isolated; a sensible location in the room plus an understanding approach from the teacher and welfare assistant can do much to make the pupil feel part of the group. If possible, it should be easy for the pupil to move into and out of the room independently; once in the room it is advantageous if the pupil has some opportunity for independent movement within the teaching area. Some pupils may require to stand for part or all of the lesson, in which case it is sensible for them to be located at the back or side of the room so as not to obstruct other pupils' view.

Pupils with learning difficulties may need guidance on where to sit, as the teacher may wish to monitor progress unobtrusively so that problems are detected and alternative teaching strategies adopted. When group work is being organized, teachers have a key role to play in deciding on the composition of such groups. By careful selection and structuring of tasks they can ensure that pupils with learning difficulties are involved. Such pupils tend to be left out of group work when free choices are made and often end up working on their own unless the teacher structures the task with care and organizes groups with sensitivity.

Acoustics

In many classrooms a certain level of working noise or 'buzz' is regarded as acceptable, particularly where pupils are searching for and using a variety of resources or where they are working on group tasks. Pupil–pupil interaction is an accepted and valuable part of a child's educational, social and emotional development and, particularly in a mixed ability situation, may well be encouraged by the teacher. In other settings peer tutoring or the 'buddy' system may be an integral part of the teaching/learning situation, again involving communication between pupils. Discovery learning techniques require pupils to work together, planning and discussing activities as they go along. For some partially hearing pupils, the level of noise generated by such teaching modes presents problems, particularly where carpeting is insufficient or absent and there are no curtains to help absorb some of the sound and cut down on echo. A traditional classroom with a wood or tiled floor instead of carpeting and window blinds instead of curtains makes it especially difficult for pupils with hearing impairment since *all* sounds are picked up and amplified by a hearing aid, and it is of course very difficult for the pupil to discern and sift out significant sounds from the confusion of noise reaching his/her ears. In a room with bare walls and with a hard floor where there is constant scraping of chairs, the teacher should made a special effort to keep pupils quiet and still while instructions are being given so that the pupil with hearing impairment can focus attention on what is being said.

A room in a building which is located beside a busy road or which opens off a noisy main school corridor presents similar difficulties for the hearing impaired, and can also cause problems for some pupils with learning difficulties who are easily distracted by noise and movement. Moreover, in much the same way as a pupil who has hearing problems will 'listen with his eyes' as well as his ears, so a pupil with visual impairment relies heavily on auditory input information in addition to using residual sight and/or specially adapted materials. Thus the key factor for a teacher to bear in mind where there are pupils with sensory handicaps present is to keep classroom noise levels to a minimum and to insist on silence when important information and directions are being given to the group as a whole. In this way, all pupils with special needs will face a minimum number of distractions at essential points during the lesson.

In some of the schools visited by the team a special unit for hearing impaired pupils had been added on after the main school was built. Wherever possible, such a unit had been sited in a quiet part of the building complex and, although this had the disadvantage of physical isolation, the undoubted benefits of a quiet teaching space were welcomed by all specialist staff to whom we spoke. Characteristically such units for the hearing impaired were carpeted, some had curtains and others in addition had some acoustic tiles to further reduce noise and echo. Staff found that a plentiful supply of power points, storage shelves and cupboards was helpful. They also appreciated the installation of furniture which could readily be rearranged for individual or group teaching purposes.

Lighting

The Vernon Report on the education of the visually handicapped stated that 'lighting is of the utmost importance to children who use sighted methods of learning' and that 'the prime consideration for schools must be to ensure that there is good general lighting and a fully adjustable system of individual lighting either at the desk or overhead' (DES, 1972, p.71). These comments and recommendations were made as a result of investigations in schools for the blind and partially sighted, but are equally apposite to pupils with visual handicap who are being educated in ordinary schools. All pupils should of course learn in rooms that are adequately lit, and additional facilities should be made available for those who are visually impaired. Different visually handicapping conditions require a range of different kinds of lighting: some pupils do not require bright light while others need a high level of illumination in which to work. In general, natural light in most ordinary schools can be supplemented by artificial sources to provide a level of illumination suitable for all pupils including those with visual impairment. Problems of glare can be controlled by the use of blinds and attention to seating arrangements, while additional lighting can be provided for individual students. Power points in classrooms were relatively few and far between, however, and sometimes lengthy extension leads were used. The latter do present a safety hazard and their use cannot be recommended.

Other considerations which should be borne in mind when classrooms are being adapted or redecorated include the following:

1. whiteboards are easier for the partially sighted to see than blackboards
2. overhead projectors are useful visual aids since they enlarge images
3. proper blackout should be available in all rooms where films and slides are shown
4. matt finish wall, ceiling and floor surfaces avoid glare and reflection
5. artificial lighting sources require regular maintenance if they are not to deteriorate in intensity and effectiveness.

As might be expected, many visually impaired pupils in the schools studied were being educated in classrooms which were far from ideal, and teachers were having to modify the physical setting in whatever way they could. One purpose-built area for the visually impaired showed what could be achieved by careful co-operative planning. This area was carpeted, had a variety of glass and painted wall surfaces and was provided with anti-dazzle window glass. Power points were installed for individual desk lamps while overhead fluorescent lights provided diffused illumination to supplement the natural daylight. Pupils with visual impairment and some with learning difficulties used this area, which proved very suitable for individual and small group tasks.

The preceding paragraphs serve to outline aspects of the physical classroom environment which help towards making this a supportive one for a pupil with special educational needs. It is evident that the preparation of the classroom in terms of decoration as well as interior fittings and furnishings is not only the responsibility of the classroom teacher but should also involve the headteacher and local authority personnel. In the chapter which follows details of the pedagogic processes which take place within these learning environments are explored.

Chapter 11
Classroom Practice

In previous chapters we have looked at different facets of the
school which impinge on the education of pupils with special
needs. The academic organization of the school, the formal
grouping of pupils, the curriculum content on offer, staffing
level and expertise all have an effect on the learning opportunities available to pupils. What happens inside the classroom,
however, affects pupils' learning most immediately, and it is the
element that is under the class teacher's direct control. Teachers
can facilitate learning within the classroom by appropriate
classroom organization, by what they teach and how they teach
it. In this chapter we look at some of the ways teachers organized
their teaching to take account of the mainstream setting. This
has been broken down into three parts, corresponding to the
main activities that teachers engage in: preparing subject
material; presenting it to pupils; and interacting with pupils to
facilitate their learning.

Preparation

For some pupils with special needs, selection of material and
preparation for a particular mode of presentation are major
considerations which may necessitate additional material or
subject modification. Often the additional work benefited other
pupils in the group whose cognitive development was at a
similar stage to that of the pupil with special needs or whose
learning style was more attuned to the different presentation.
    One task of preparation is to identify key concepts and basic

information necessary to understanding the subject as a whole. Many teachers recorded this kind of information in the form of duplicated handouts to ensure that the concepts discussed in a lesson were grasped by pupils and retained accurately. Teachers found such handouts to be of particular value to some pupils with special needs although modification often had to be made in their preparation.

Many pupils with moderate learning difficulties were able to engage in the work done by the rest of their class if it was prepared in a simple form and individualized instructions were available. Such pupils coped better with handouts prepared in print or capital letters rather than in cursive writing. As well as the usual handouts and work cards prepared for the class, an additional sheet containing key words with a simple explanation of their meaning, commensurate with the pupil's level of understanding, was found to be useful. A simple example of this technique is shown in this extract from a handout given to pupils with moderate learning difficulties participating in a mixed ability science lesson: '. . . most materials expand (grow bigger) when heated and contract (grow smaller) when cooled . . .' Step-by-step descriptions of how to perform experiments were also available to pupils with special needs at the same school. During practical lessons the pupils worked with peers of higher ability, and as well as their own work cards had access to textbooks used by the rest of the class. The work cards simplified the instructions given in the textbook and often included simplified diagrams. They also included a list of items needed for the experiment and any safety rules relating to it. Having carried out the experiment, pupils wrote up what they did with the aid of an information card which specified the information that the teacher wanted the pupil to record accurately and a structure within which to record it. An illustrated information card on Getting Water Back is as follows:

1) Write down today's date and the title.
2) Copy the information from page 17 in the textbook.
3) Copy out the diagram (given on the card)
4) Copy out the following sentences, fill in the missing words.

... We put some ink in an evaporating dish and heated it. When steam came from the ink we put a beaker over it for a few seconds. We found ... on the inside of the beaker. This ... has come from the ink.

Although this preparation involved the class teacher in additional time and effort, the material accrued was found to be useful for other groups of pupils at the school such as hearing impaired pupils. A hearing impaired pupil, dependent on lipreading, cannot take notes *and* watch the teacher's lips, and will therefore benefit from a prepared handout summarizing the lesson content. Also the reduced language experience of many hearing impaired pupils means that they have difficulties with syntax and may confuse the meaning of sentences, so the simple explanations given in the work cards helped to ensure that they recorded work accurately.

Visually impaired pupils present other problems for the teacher preparing lessons. For example, a pupil who can read print material may not be able to cope with the size of print found in most texts or work cards. For these pupils enlarged print materials will have to be ordered in advance. As few class teachers were responsible for ordering such materials them-selves, this often entailed considerable liaison with a specialist or designated teacher.

Many class teachers who taught visually impaired pupils within an ordinary class felt initially that everything they might need for the lesson had to be enlarged. As one teacher explained, until she received feedback from pupils she was never sure which of several texts she was going to require. She planned her programme on a weekly basis and gave everything that might need enlargement to the peripatetic teacher. However, as teachers got to know their pupils, it became obvious that certain texts had a style appropriate to individual pupils' learning and teachers restricted the enlargement requirements to these texts without detriment to the lesson flow. Thus in the early stages of accommodating pupils with visual impairments teachers tended to over-prepare. For most schools such over-preparation was not wasted as they had a continuing intake of visually impaired pupils who could benefit from the additional material. The materials prepared by a class teacher were generally stored and kept accessible to other class teachers so that as time went on the need for new preparation was reduced.

For the blind pupil, or the partially sighted one who is a braille reader, appropriate braille texts and materials have to be acquired. As there is not a wealth of braille material available, teachers were generally restricted to the texts available. In some instances brailling of specific texts for examination subjects was carried out. This could take considerable time so that long term planning was necessary.

As an alternative strategy, or when appropriate braille materials were not available, some class teachers prepared tapes of set books or dictated lesson notes for use by the blind pupil after the lesson. Such preparation was time-consuming, but a library of taped material could be built up and made available to other pupils whose learning style depended more on an auditory mode than a visual mode. The Royal National Institute for the Blind (RNIB) was found to be a useful source of taped books for blind pupils.

Many teachers commented that planning lessons for pupils with special needs in mind had forced them to think through the material more and plan accordingly, to the benefit of all pupils in the class. Much of the material prepared was not pupil specific and could be used for the benefit of other pupils. For example, a number of teachers found that models which had been prepared so that visually impaired pupils could handle them helped sighted pupils also to grasp abstract concepts more easily. The use of models in this way is explained more fully in the next section.

Presentation

If the ability of pupils within a group is similar, a particular structuring and sequencing of material may be appropriate for all members of the class. However, because of differences in learning styles of individual pupils, it is usually necessary to present material in a variety of ways. Dunn (1963) concludes that the immediate environment can produce a biological reaction in some pupils that can hinder or improve learning, depending upon whether or not the learning style of the pupil is accommodated.

The inclusion of pupils with special needs in mainstream classes has forced many teachers to rethink their mode of presentation to the benefit of many other pupils. Blind or severely partially sighted pupils tend to approach abstract conceptualization problems from the concrete and functional level, and consequently may lag behind their sighted peers. Additional manipulative and exploratory activities which had been afforded to blind/partially sighted pupils were also found to benefit pupils with learning difficulties. Pupils with moderate learning difficulties can cope with much subject material, even at secondary stage, if it is presented at the concrete level. One secondary school found that many such pupils could work along with the rest of the class when they were able to manipulate materials. For example, in science basic principles of electricity and electrical circuits were understood if pupils could handle concrete objects. They were also allowed to represent their experiments as drawings rather than in symbolic diagrams. When presented with the same material in the usual symbolic way, as in circuit diagrams, these pupils completely failed to grasp the concepts. Where it is not possible to present subject material in a three dimensional form, there may be scope to present visual material in an enlarged or simplified form.

Programmes of work involving simultaneous tactile activities were provided for blind pupils. For example, in one mainstream secondary school the biology teacher presented a blind pupil with a simple tactile diagram made from solder wire while sighted pupils were presented with visual diagrams. When new concepts or materials were being introduced the pupil sat next to the teacher who guided her fingers over the diagram while explaining the material to the class. Tactile maps were available in geography and were presented in a similar manner. Mathematical concepts were also presented in a tactile way, e.g. graph work using a plastic sheet and raised graph grids. Cork boards and aluminium foil (RNIB) together with braille rulers were used for teaching measuring. Spatial topics (e.g. volume and angles) caused considerable problems, and it was planned to obtain a variety of solid models for the mathematics department so that the basic concepts could be presented from the outset in a tactile mode.

As blind pupils pass through all stages of Piagetian development, but generally at an age later than sighted pupils, it is advisable that new concepts be presented at the concrete level (Gough, 1981). Indeed new concepts may elude blind pupils unless they have experienced them in this way. It is particularly helpful if a visually impaired pupil can manipulate models during their construction. For instance, at a mainstream secondary school the visually impaired pupils were encouraged to manipulate models at each stage of construction in order that increased understanding of the working of the model was gained. In some instances the tactile instruction must be carefully carried out as not all materials are pleasant to feel. Manipulation of materials was more common at primary than secondary level, despite the fact that many secondary pupils could benefit from a tactile/kinaesthetic approach. Other pupils also benefited from a tactile approach, particularly when new vocabulary was introduced. Many mainstream teachers encouraged such pupils to manipulate materials particularly when introducing new concepts or descriptive words.

It may be necessary to alter the focus of the material in order to get a particular concept over to a pupil. Certain visual concepts such as light, colour and reflection may have to be tackled in quite a different way for visually impaired pupils. The science teacher at one primary school planned some lessons on shadows, using heat lamps for the visually impaired pupils instead of lights. If a school is particularly well equipped light sensors may be used in some experiments. Teachers found, particularly with lower age groups, that the use of simultaneous audio/tactile and visual inputs paid dividends for other pupils, especially those still needing to approach new concepts from a concrete level. Many such techniques are appropriate to a wide range of subject areas.

For pupils with hearing impairment or learning difficulties many teachers have found it appropriate to repeat instructions or present material directly to the pupils concerned immediately after whole class instruction. In a large class such a strategy may be difficult to carry out without constant distractions or interruptions. To ensure that a pupil was not held up, many teachers assigned a 'friend' so that the pupil could start individual or group work and proceed until the teacher could spend time with him/her.

In fact, several teachers found that, in large mixed ability classes, organizing the class into co-operative working groups resulted in improved pupil motivation and increased the participation of all pupils. Group working is not new to many practical subjects, although structuring the group so that each member has a particular responsibility is probably a new dimension of group working for many teachers, particularly at secondary level. Such a group would contain four or five pupils, each assigned an achievable responsibility for the task in hand using their best skill. Such groups have been used with success in a mainstream primary school with several hearing impaired pupils in role. The structuring of the groups has emphasized the value of each class member and prevented isolation of those with a disability. When interviewed, teachers spoke of their initial concern over the amount of time involved in setting up the groups and the lack of progress in programmes of work. Once groups were stabilized, however, pupils were found to work well together and to produce more work, of higher quality and with increased understanding. Such group structuring was used experimentally for one term with first year classes at a mainstream secondary school having a large number of pupils with a variety of special needs on roll. Such was the success of the venture, with the progress of pupils with moderate learning difficulties being particularly commented upon, that the school planned to extend the practice.

The rise of co-operative working groups enabled teachers to present material to the whole class, adapting the style where necessary for pupils with particular needs but not needing to reiterate instructions directly to individual pupils. One teacher felt that the practice made it easier to accommodate pupils with special needs into mainstream classes. Pupils were better motivated, had a clearer understanding of what they should be doing and spent more time on task.

Many pupils with moderate learning difficulties have problems with abstract concepts. One secondary school, convinced that the curriculum for these pupils should include basic science concepts, was experimenting with a concept analysis approach to teaching science in mixed ability groups. The approach fosters concept formation, thinking ability, logical deduction and creative problem solving and is of course a viable approach to use with non-handicapped pupils. The scheme had been in use for one term with outstanding success and it was hoped to extend it in future terms.

The approach revolves around identifying critical and non-critical attributes of the concept to be taught. The teacher concerned has to develop an instructional plan based on five phases. This is exemplified below by the plan used to teach the concept 'mammals'.

PHASE 1   The concept is identified

PHASE 2   The concept is analysed with the class. The pupils are invited to state their ideas on how to identify 'mammals'. The teacher lists all their ideas dividing them into: critical (peculiar to mammals) and non-critical, e.g.

Critical	*Non-critical*
Body covered with fur	Colour
Mammary gland	Size
Birth of live young	Age
Limbs based on a	Feeding
pentadactyl pattern	Lifespan

PHASE 3   The teacher with help from the class identifies examples and non-examples of the concept. (These teaching strategies are well known to science teachers but next two phases promote the concept in a manner likely to make the internalizing of the concept easier for the pupil.)

PHASE 4   The teacher presents examples and non-examples. To be really effective this has to be done in a variety of ways, e.g. live specimens, pictures, models, in large numbers and in a variety of situations. For pupils with moderate learning difficulties it is essential that they build up a mastery of examples before non-examples are introduced.

PHASE 5   The teacher presents finer levels of discrimination. Initially the differences between examples and non-examples are great. As the pupils master the clear contrasts they are required to make finer discrimination e.g. going from man as an example and rock as a non-example to ant-eater as an example and armadillo as a non-example.

Because techniques of co-operative group working and concept analysis approach are extensions of strategies already known and used by many class teachers, schools experimenting with their use have found them relatively easy to introduce.

Teacher-pupil interaction

Having prepared appropriate materials and presented them to the class, the teacher must then facilitate pupils' learning by asking questions of individual pupils, promoting discussion and generally engaging in verbal interaction with them. We examined this in terms of the frequency with which such interaction took place, the comprehensibility of the language used and the nature of any reinforcement given.

Teacher-pupil contacts vary greatly in frequency, not only between classrooms but also within classrooms, and inevitably some pupils attract more teaching attention than others. In observed classrooms pupils with special needs often had less contact with their teachers for instructional purposes than did their peers. The frequency of interaction reflected the teacher's perception of the need for the pupil to be given further guidance or information. Some pupils did not initiate many teacher-pupil interactions that would enable teachers to check their understanding. Their particular needs and difficulties with learning often went unnoticed for some time or until their written work revealed problems.

This was well illustrated in one secondary school catering for a large number of hearing impaired pupils. These often gave the impression of comprehending more than they did. They keenly observed their peers and imitated them, for example raising their hands when other pupils did and going along with activities without really understanding what they were doing. As mainstream staff were likely to have thirty other pupils they were often not aware that the hearing impaired pupil was imitating and not understanding. It was only through regular interaction with pupils that it was possible to find out how much they were understanding. Again, visually impaired pupils sometimes went to great lengths to conceal their difficulties from teachers and classmates. Some pupils we observed did not acknowledge problems in reading from the board or from poorly duplicated sheets, preferring instead to rely on their neighbours for help. Often incorrect copying led to problems with lesson content and understanding of concepts that were not apparent without close observation and questioning by the teacher.

At times the teacher may choose to make fewer demands on a pupil, feeling that to do so may put undue pressure on or embarrass the pupil. This was particularly so with pupils having difficulties orally because of poor speech or language development. Pupils who are unable or unwilling to answer questions or ask for help but sit quietly in class often escape the notice of the class teacher. Many teachers remarked that pupils with special needs, particularly hearing impaired pupils, would say that they understood what was going on, yet their written work revealed misinformation and general lack of understanding.

Once a pattern of reduced interactions between pupil and teacher is established it may be difficult for the mainstream teacher to appreciate that lower expectations are being operated for these pupils, and as a result the opportunities for verbal interaction may diminish further. Of the pupils with special needs, those with sensory loss were least likely to initiate teacher contact. Their normally quiet and seemingly attentive behaviour did not make undue demands on teacher time. Also, many teachers who took particular care to ensure that these pupils had understood the directions given argued that further questioning and interaction would draw too much attention to the pupil and could have a detrimental effect on their motivation. There is certainly a need for teachers to learn to be sensitive to a pupil's willingness to be drawn into conversation, since too much questioning when the pupil is feeling insecure will merely discourage him/her from further spontaneous conversation. From our observations pupils with physical handicaps had similar interactions with teachers as their peers, particularly in terms of instructional conversation. The main difference for this group lay in the fact that the teacher tended to approach the pupil and therefore initiate the interaction. More frequent verbal demands were made on physically handicapped pupils, and teachers were more aware of any difficulties these pupils encountered than with pupils with sensory impairments or learning difficulties. This may be due to the fact that teacher expectations of academic progress for pupils with physical handicaps were higher than for other pupils with special needs.

As we have seen, the interaction between a pupil with special needs and the class teacher was often limited, with the result that the teacher's ability to assess the pupil's progress accurately during the lesson was significantly reduced. Antisocial or avoidance behaviour also masked situations where pupils with special needs were confused or afraid of appearing stupid. This was particularly true of hearing impaired pupils who were conscious of their deficient speech and preferred to stay in the background.

It may be necessary, particularly when the language skills of the pupil are somewhat less than those of their peers, to phrase a question simply or to reiterate concepts presented during class in a more simplified way. Teachers are used to adapting written work to meet the needs of pupils yet often forget to make the necessary adjustments when speaking.

Insisting on technical language or 'language of the secondary school' can also discourage pupils from responding, particularly those pupils who have difficulty in framing questions or answers. It may be necessary to encourage these pupils by frequent use of 'everyday' language, using words understood by the pupil. From this basis, new and more technical words can be introduced gradually and at frequency reflecting the pupil's ability to cope.

The type of questioning used by teachers is also important. Many teachers used 'closed' questioning frequently, when they expected only one answer. This type of questioning is discouraging to many pupils who would benefit from greater use of open-ended questions which would allow them to explore their own ideas and come up with a variety of possible solutions. The possibility of giving a 'wrong' answer to an open ended question is less than for a 'closed' question, and encourages pupils to verbalize their ideas rather more. On the basis of the language produced in this way the teacher can then see if further guidance is required for the pupil to internalize the concept accurately.

A critical factor in any learning situation is the nature and pacing of reinforcement. As learning progresses there is a shift away from extrinsic (e.g. teacher praise) to intrinsic (e.g. solving a problem for its own sake) reinforcement. At secondary level, even when extrinsic reward is given, it is often deferred. Many pupils with special educational needs, particularly those with moderate learning difficulties, require the use of immediate extrinsic reinforcement for a longer period of time. Many teachers remarked on the seeming inability of pupils to work without this constant reassurance that they were doing 'the right thing'. Some pupils do need to be weaned away from dependence on constant teacher reinforcement, but such a process has to be gradual and requires considerable understanding on the part of teachers. It was probably in this respect that pupils with special needs differed most obviously from their peers, and the need for constant reinforcement was a source of considerable frustration to teachers, particularly at secondary level.

Teachers also seemed to have difficulty in balancing rewards to pupils with special needs, giving praise somewhat indiscriminately or hardly at all. However, if the balance was wrong it led to frustration or withdrawal on the part of the pupil. Since appropriate reinforcement is an important factor in a learning situation greater attention needs to be paid to it.

Chapter 12
Monitoring Progress

The final stage in the teaching process is evaluation. Teachers must take stock of the learning situations they create and assess how well they are meeting their teaching objectives. This entails monitoring pupil progress, both in the short term through feedback obtained in the course of a lesson and on a longer term basis by means of tests and records of various kinds.

Such monitoring of progress is no less important for pupils with special needs than for other pupils. Indeed, it becomes all the more important in their case because of the complexity of their teaching needs and because their programmes of work are often individualized, and cut across the school's mainstream arrangements. For these reasons mainstream monitoring arrangements even when adequate in their own right may not suffice for these pupils. This chapter reports on the arrangements schools made for monitoring the progress of pupils with special needs. An initial problem is the frequent complexity of their programming in relation to the mainstream curriculum. This means that it is important to have clear lines of responsibility for overseeing their progress. Much of the formal monitoring was done through use of records of various kinds and through meetings, and these are considered next. Finally in this chapter, we look at the special allowances and accommodations made for pupils with special needs and how these impinged on monitoring their progress.

Responsibility for monitoring progress

Responsibility for monitoring the progress of pupils with special needs was generally vested in the teacher in charge of special needs, where such existed in the school. This function of the designated teacher has been described in chapter 7. A particular task was to collate information from the different teachers responsible for a given pupil. This in turn required the designated teacher to ensure that staff did monitor pupils' progress and recorded appropriate information on them. This necessitated good liaison between staff, and in some cases assisting mainstream teachers to develop appropriate monitoring procedures for use in their classes.

A particular question regarding responsibility for monitoring arose when pupils were dividing their time between a special school and an ordinary school. It was generally agreed by staff involved that monitoring procedures should be worked out before the pupil links started. In schools where links were established, a teacher from each school was designated as the link person, coordinating activities each within his or her own school and responsible for any liaison necessary between the schools. The role of the link teacher was to coordinate the programme of work for the pupils concerned and to ensure their progress in the subject areas studied in the separate schools. Each link teacher was also responsible for ensuring that staff involved in the programmes had any help and materials they needed and were clear on monitoring procedures.

Occasionally staff from the special schools were able to support the mainstream classes attended by their pupils and provide an additional source of information to the link teachers about pupil progress. This occurred at one comprehensive school which catered for several hearing impaired pupils from the local special school for the deaf. In addition, the hearing impaired pupils attending mainstream classes in the first three years carried notebooks, which were initialled by the teacher after each lesson. Staff were encouraged to write comments about work covered, progress made and any notable features of behaviour and to indicate written homework given. The notebooks were checked by the link teachers at the special school on a weekly basis and daily by the link teacher at the comprehensive. This procedure ensured that all staff concerned with the pupils knew what work had been covered, allowed staff to deal with problems as they arose and ensured pupils were coping with the mainstream work.

Records

Educational records were a principal means by which teachers monitored progress and many monitoring procedures involved careful documentation of work done and progress made. The arrangements made for documenting and recording information about pupils with special needs tended to be more formal than for other pupils. Sometimes special record cards were provided for staff to fill in on a daily or weekly basis.

It must be remembered that record keeping is simply a means to an end, and therefore the system devised should be relevant to those staff who are to use it. There should be agreement amongst staff on the types of records to be kept by the school as a whole, otherwise record keeping is likely to be pushed aside (Shipman, 1983). It is worth deciding from the outset who are to be the primary users, and the kind of information that is required. Devising a comprehensive system that is too sophisticated to use or which results in wasted effort because the records remain unread by those for whom they were intended is counterproductive.

Records generally had to be completed in the teacher's own time, although designated teachers sometimes had a timetabled slot for administrative tasks which could be given over to record keeping. In order to reduce the burden of work associated with maintaining detailed records some schools preferred to document work covered and progress made no more than twice a term. Special forms were provided for this purpose and circulated to staff concerned at appropriate intervals. The format did not vary a great deal from school to school. Example 1 illustrates the pattern.

Several schools had forms designed to help the class teacher monitor pupil progress on a lesson by lesson basis. By drawing together the information obtained in this way, schools were also able to evaluate subject content and pupil progress over a long period of time. In some schools such forms or record cards were used only for pupils with special needs, whereas in others class teachers were encouraged to keep such records for all pupils. These records document not only what was taught but also how the pupil coped and what progress was made. The design of such a form is illustrated in example 2.

EXAMPLE 1

Subject	Work covered	Progress/ comments	Date

Name . . . .   Date . . . .
Form . . . .   Date of birth . . . .

EXAMPLE 2

Pupil's name			Form			
PROGRAMME			RECORD			
Material to be used	Instructions to pupils	Expected pupil behaviour	Criteria for successful task completion	Date worked on	Date com- pleted	Date check

Such records made clear exactly what the pupil was working on, the way he/she was to work and when the material was successfully mastered. They also helped staff to identify areas of weakness in sufficient detail for help to be given as needed. Permanent records of ongoing and previous work mastered were particularly useful to teachers new to the group or covering for an absent colleague. Teachers aiming to provide a balanced programme of work found the overview contained in record cards such as these particularly useful, and in any case some sort of record keeping was needed to ensure continuity.

In schools which had very few pupils with special needs on roll, teachers tended to keep less formal written records. These generally took the form of log books in which teachers noted classroom activities for the day or week and any progress made by individual pupils. For example, in one primary school which had a special class for pupils with moderate learning difficulties, staff used a log book to record all pupil activities whether in the special class or in the mainstream. In order to keep the special class teacher in touch with pupils' work, mainstream teachers recorded the work covered in their classes and commented on any difficulties. The special class teacher in turn wrote down what was being done in the unit, often offering suggestions for appropriate materials that could be used in mainstream. This log book provided a permanent record of pupil activity and provided a basis on which staff met from time to time in order to discuss the future needs of the pupils.

To reduce the amount of time spent by the teacher in keeping records up to date there is the possibility of involving the pupils themselves. Indeed it is already fairly common practice for pupils to mark their own class tests. This gives the teacher the opportunity to discuss errors with the pupil and can lead to pupils contributing towards their own records. None of the schools in the study had in fact opened up record keeping by pupils in this way. A number of authors (Foster, 1971; Davies, 1980; Shipman, 1983) draw attention to this means of building up records and point to the benefits for pupils and teacher alike from adopting it.

Meetings

In some schools, meetings to review the progress of pupils with special needs were arranged on a formal basis and were part of the school timetable. Thus, weekly staff meetings were arranged in some schools so that all staff involved with pupils having special needs could come together to discuss work done, materials used and problems arising. When a school had on roll a large number of pupils with special needs not all pupils could be discussed at each meeting. A common tactic in this situation was to limit the number of pupils to be discussed formally at a given meeting, selecting those that were discussed on a rota basis so that individuals were not neglected. One primary school operating in this way was able to ensure that each pupil was discussed at least twice a term, but by limiting the number of pupils there was time in the weekly meeting to consider other pupils causing immediate concern.

Not all schools could arrange weekly meetings between staff but encouraged designated teachers to attend department meetings at which course content and materials were discussed. Most designated teachers found that attending these meetings helped them keep in touch with the work being done in mainstream. As such meetings tended to be held every three to four weeks they did not take up too much of the designated teacher's time.

In addition to the meetings described above some schools also arranged case conferences for all pupils with special needs. These were usually held once a year when all the information about each pupil was collated and discussed by staff concerned with the pupil. The purpose of the case conference was to review the progress made in the course of the year and to plan for the future needs of the pupil. The meetings also served to bring together teachers, other professionals such as educational psychologists and school medical officers, and – in some cases – parents, to enable a comprehensive picture of the pupil to be built up.

Making allowances

Pupils with special needs were generally allowed much longer than peers to complete written assignments, be these class work, homework or written examinations. Such pupils often take considerably longer to complete written and/or reading tasks than their peers. The visually impaired pupil may have problems which cannot be wholly corrected with spectacles or magnifying aids. The pupil with defects in the right hand area of the visual field is unable to read quickly as he/she cannot scan ahead when reading from left to right as a person with normal vision does. Pupils with macular damage (fine detail) have difficulty with small print or complicated diagrams and the severely myopic pupil even with magnifying aids may only be able to cope with one letter at a time. Copying from sheets or the board is difficult and time-consuming for many pupils with special needs. The physically handicapped pupil may find the task of writing slow and laborious, and for these pupils and some visually impaired pupils the standard of written work produced may be poor. To improve the clarity of the work produced, such pupils were encouraged to use typewriters; although their use did enable pupils to work more quickly they still required longer than peers to do work set.

When more time was allowed for pupils to complete written tasks there tended to be a subsequent delay before the work was handed in. As a result, the work was often marked separately from the rest of the group. Class teachers were concerned that different standards might be applied to the marking of work handed in separately and later than the rest of the group. For this reason they tended to favour the tactic of requiring the pupil with special needs to complete less work or selected items only rather than having them complete all class work but over a longer period.

Sometimes it was not the pupils who required extra time to complete work, but the specialist teacher who needed time to prepare work for the class teacher. An example is the need for a specialist teacher to overwrite braille work before it can be marked by the class teachers. When there was a need for transcribing work, specialist staff involved tried to ensure that any delays in getting pupils' work back to the class teacher were as few and short as possible. Some time lapse was inevitable, and there was a need for planning and liaison between staff involved.

Written work is important, as it indicates not only the level of understanding of the pupil and progress being made but also strengths and weaknesses in pupil–teacher interactions. Pupils unable or unwilling to answer questions or ask for help but who sit quietly in class often escape the notice of the class teacher. It is only when written work is handed in that areas of weakness are revealed. For those pupils designated as having special needs the standard of acceptability of written work was often lower, and on many occasions their work was observed to be marked more leniently than that of other class members. (When interviewed, many teachers qualified statements about pupil progress and achievement with the remark 'for a handicapped pupil'.) For this reason, it is important that information about pupil progress recorded by class teachers should be collated by the teacher responsible for special needs, who would then have assembled the best available information on each pupil's response to the educational programming being offered.

Chapter 13
Use of Second Adult and Pupil Helpers in the Classroom

Class teachers' efforts can be supplemented by the judicious use of additional help in the classroom. Such help is sometimes the deciding factor in enabling an individual pupil to join a mainstream lesson. In the schools studied this help was provided, in different ways, by teachers, by ancillary staff and by other pupils.

Second teacher in the classroom

A small number of schools made use of a second teacher to provide support in mainstream classes. This was in all cases a specialist teacher of pupils with special needs. The aim was to allow the mainstream teacher to proceed at a normal pace while ensuring that the pupil with special needs participated fully in the lesson.

The arrangements made varied considerably in practice but they can be viewed as falling into three types:
1. Second teacher working wholly with the pupil with special needs
2. Second teacher working mainly with the pupil with special needs but available to help other pupils as well
3. Second teacher working with a small group of pupils within the class which might or might not include the pupil with special needs.

In all cases observed, the mainstream teacher continued to be responsible for organizing the lesson and preparing and presenting materials, and remained in overall charge of the class.

1. *Working only with pupils with special needs*

Many of the schools using a second teacher in a mainstream class initially scheduled the teacher to work exclusively with a specific pupil. They had found that class teachers could not give adequate attention to some pupils while teaching the rest of the class, so that additional teaching support was necessary. When this took the form of a second teacher for a given pupil, it was clear that the pupil had a far better opportunity of participating in the lesson. The role of the second teacher grew out of this situation as class teachers gained confidence in working with a second teacher present.

One mainstream school, catering for hearing impaired pupils from a neighbouring special school, received teaching support from special school staff. The support teacher, who might or might not be a subject specialist, was scheduled to support the hearing impaired pupil in designated lessons. After the class teacher introduced the lesson, the support teacher tended to work exclusively with the hearing impaired pupils, helping them with written work or with specified exercises. In lessons where pupils read aloud the support teacher sat by the hearing impaired pupils and pointed to the text with his/her finger. In some subject areas the hearing impaired pupils were able to cope on their own and, with the agreement of the class teacher, the support teacher would give assistance to other members of the class as required. The support teachers were able to ensure that the pupils understood the lesson and could interpret for the pupils or class teacher if a problem in communication arose. They were also able to monitor the progress of the hearing impaired pupils and their ability to cope with lesson content and presentation. A drawback in this particular situation was that support could only be provided when special school staff were available, so that the timing – and the nature – of support was determined by teacher availability rather than pupil need. A positive factor was that teachers did follow-up work with integrating pupils when they returned to the special school, and being present at lessons enabled them to do the follow-up work more effectively.

2. *Working with pupils with special needs and others*

Another school having a unit for partial hearing pupils on site was able to organize in-class support by specialist teachers from the unit. The scheme began by using the unit staff for those areas of the curriculum pertinent to their subject specialism, while in mainstream classes the unit staff not only helped the hearing impaired pupils but any other pupils requiring teacher assistance. This type of support had the full co-operation of the mainstream teachers concerned. Before unit staff joined mainstream lessons the co-operating staff discussed the needs of the hearing impaired pupils and mainstream teachers' expectations of the lessons.

Support by unit staff was given in science, maths, history and geography. Supporting mainstream staff in this way was a new development for the school. It was constrained by the limited amount of time unit staff could devote to it. All staff concerned felt that the presence of unit staff in lessons was a good point of contact between them. It also gave unit staff the chance to monitor pupil progress in mainstream lessons.

When providing support, unit staff gave priority to the hearing impaired pupils, ensuring that they understood the work and could get on with it. Thereafter, the unit teacher gave help to other pupils requiring it. One mainstream teacher when interviewed felt that the scheme was excellent in that it ensured maximum teacher time for all pupils and the group could benefit from having two subject specialists present. Other staff supported the view that increased staff presence was of benefit to all pupils.

3. *Second teacher taking a group of pupils within a mainstream class*

This strategy, which often expanded into team teaching, was commonly found in primary schools, probably reflecting prevailing teaching liaised with the class teacher prior to the lesson, and would often work with a particular group of pupils according to the needs of the class. This group might or might not contain pupils with special needs. The class teacher would introduce the lesson and organize the work, after which each teacher tended to work with a particular group. Both teachers, when not involved with their own group, would keep an eye on the rest of the class.

The use of a second teacher to work with groups of pupils developed in some instances into team teaching. This occurred at a primary school having some visually handicapped pupils on roll. The specialist teacher worked alongside the class teacher as part of the teaching team. Her presence in the mainstream class meant that any difficulty with a visually impaired pupil could be resolved immediately. A bonus was that the mainstream teacher could observe how a specialist teacher worked with a visually impaired pupil.

However a second teacher was used, the mainstream teacher still prepared and presented materials in an appropriate manner using the principles described in the previous section. The presence of a second teacher meant that pupil/teacher interaction would be maximized, giving a more accurate evaluation of pupil progress than could often be obtained when a class teacher was working alone. Class materials and subject presentation were discussed by the co-operating teachers and any modifications necessary were then made by the class teacher.

Ancillaries in the classroom

The research team identified two main educational roles for ancillaries in mainstream classes: working alongside a specific pupil, and carrying out general duties while having a watching brief on a specific pupil. In practice, the work carried out was dependent on the subject, the requirements of the mainstream teacher and the needs of the pupils concerned.

It was policy in many schools that an ancillary would accompany a pupil with special needs who was joining a mainstream class for the first time. The presence of the ancillary in these circumstances gave confidence to pupil and class teacher alike. During these initial periods, when a pupil with special needs was introduced to a mainstream class, the ancillary tended to confine herself to that pupil. As the pupil became established in the class, the ancillary became more available to the rest of the class. How the ancillary worked depended on the pupil's specific difficulties and the subject area involved. For example, visually and physically impaired pupils tended to need more help in PE, art and craft, while pupils with learning difficulties or hearing impairments tended to need help in more academic areas such as reading and written work. It must be emphasized, however, that the subject areas presenting difficulty varied considerably from pupil to pupil, and did not follow directly from particular handicapping conditions.

When they worked almost exclusively with particular pupils, ancillary staff had to refrain from doing the work for them. These pupils were in the mainstream in order to be encouraged to work for themselves and to become as mentally and physically independent as their specific difficulties would allow. The deployment of an ancillary bought time, as it were, to further this process – time a class teacher could not afford to give – and it was imperative that the opportunity should not be wasted through a narrow focus on producing neat and correct work.

This role of ancillary staff in guiding and encouraging pupils with special needs was observed many times. Pupils with physical handicaps, particularly if the handicap was severe, were often allocated an ancillary full time. In many cases the ancillary was observed to act as a guide, assisting the pupil in a very unobtrusive way and giving the pupil ideas on how to use equipment involved in class work. In an observed cookery lesson the ancillary assisted the pupil in much this way. The ancillary did not help or correct the pupil but merely guided, making helpful suggestions, for example, "If you leave the packet there you can see the instructions," "I think you need turn the oven on now" and, with regard to the pupil's wheelchair which was being negotiated between oven and worktop, "Try to get in a position where you don't need to move about all the time". The pupil had use of only one hand and was finding it difficult to work, so the ancillary tried to ensure she made the best use of any residual motor skills by spending lengthy periods of time practising new skills with her. In one lesson the pupil was using a spatula for the first time, so the ancillary spent time going over the required motor movements until the idea was successfully transmitted. A class teacher could not give sufficient time to ensure that such a pupil learned new skills in this way. The class teacher did come over from time to time to see how pupil and ancillary were progressing, and to make suggestions as to what they might do next or how they might adapt the recipe or instructions. This teacher spent time before and after the lesson discussing with the ancillary ways and means of adapting each stage of the work to the needs of the pupil.

A subject obviously requiring the use of motor skills is PE, and the team observed the use of ancillaries in these lessons. Occasionally the ancillary merely ensured that the pupil was in the best position to take part in the lesson. At other times she took the pupil through the range of movements required, ensuring that they were carried out correctly, as in dance or keep fit activities. Sometimes it was necessary, as with a hearing impaired pupil, to ensure that all instructions had been understood. Several pupils observed were unable to cope with recording their own work and had an ancillary with them for this purpose. The ancillaries emphasized the need to record only what the pupil indicated and not to correct the work in any way. This was felt essential to enable the class teacher to know the difficulties being encountered by the pupil.

Ancillaries played an important role in facilitating pupils' work by ensuring that they understood what was to be done. For visually impaired pupils this might require the ancillary to copy work from texts or board in a suitable way for the pupil to use. For pupils with learning difficulties the work had often to be translated into very simple terms on to a worksheet that the pupil could have alongside him or her. Hearing impaired pupils sometimes missed verbal instructions or details and it was up to the ancillary to fill in the gaps.

At other times, particularly at primary level, ancillaries would work alongside pupils hearing them read, talking to them about what they had read and encouraging speech. Often the ancillary was able to provide back-up language and vocabulary work at a level at which it was rarely possible for a class teacher to provide. This type of support was particularly important for young pupils with hearing impairment.

At one primary school where several pupils with learning difficulties were in a mainstream class an ancillary provided fairly constant support. One pupil in particular required a great deal of help and was observed to refer constantly to the ancillary and to be reluctant to work unless closely supervised by her. This pupil benefited from social contact with mainstream pupils and the presence of the ancillary helped to ensure his academic progress without putting undue demands on the class teacher's time.

In some situations where it was necessary for an ancillary to work closely with the pupil in this way, class teachers commented that they often did not know when and how often to check up on a pupil's progress. However, the team observed that when pupils had problems with lesson content the ancillary working with them encouraged the pupil to ask the class teacher for help. This was felt to be essential to enable the pupil to get to know the teacher and to allow the teacher to become aware of difficulties encountered.

Once established in a class, it was not always necessary for an ancillary to work exclusively with a pupil, and intermittent attention allied to checking progress was all that was necessary. While carrying out a monitoring role, the ancillary often did odd jobs for the class teacher such as checking library books, distributing materials, helping generally in practical lessons or hearing other pupils read. Occasionally the ancillary would work with a group of pupils engaged in a specific task within the classroom, for instance, model making or painting, but was still available to monitor the pupil with special needs and give assistance if required. The ancillary would report back to the class teacher and/or the specialist teacher on any areas of difficulty observed which would have otherwise gone unnoticed in a large class. The need for a watching brief was emphasized by staff in one primary school. In this school pupils with severe physical and learning difficulties attended mainstream classes as much as possible. They instanced one pupil who appeared to be coping well in a mainstream class but whose difficulties with subject content went largely unnoticed for a considerable time. It was not until the arrival of an ancillary in the group, for another pupil, that staff were alerted to the difficulties.

Many teachers felt that ancillary staff could be used far more in classrooms, at both primary and secondary levels, without detracting from the independence of the pupil. Their presence would ensure maximum lesson participation by pupils with special needs and provide teachers with an extra pair of 'eyes' or 'hands', alerting them to difficulties which might otherwise go unnoticed and enabling pupils to receive a degree of individual attention not otherwise possible.

Use of pupil helpers

Non-handicapped pupils were used to give help and assistance in a variety of ways. The pupil helper might be from the designated pupil's own class or from an older group. Such helpers were referred to by different titles such as 'pals', 'pupil helpers', 'peer tutors' or simply 'friends'. Classmates offering help either did so spontaneously or were assigned to pupils with special needs on a rota system. The latter was often used at primary level and guarded against changes in friendship groups, and was particularly useful when a pupil with special needs first joined a class.

The assistance given may be of a purely logistical kind, in setting up equipment such as lights, typewriters, special tables or chairs or in fetching the necessary materials to complete class exercises as in science lessons. The helper may have the responsibility of ensuring that the pupil has appropriate notes from lessons by loaning his/her notes or by making a copy of them.

During the part of the lesson when pupils are writing up information or carrying out exercises or experiments, the helper was often observed to clarify what the teacher had said by repeating or enlarging on it. Such help enabled the teacher to ensure that everyone in the class was getting on before coming over to the designated pupil to check on progress. It also allowed the teacher to use standard verbal expressions and means of presenting material. Many teachers remarked that when they selected helpers they opted for pupils of average ability. It was felt that the average pupil tended to make more detailed notes from which to write up information. Bright pupils by contrast needed fewer memory prompts; their notes might consist of single words or phrases rather than sentences and as such were not particularly helpful to some pupils with special needs, in particular hearing impaired pupils.

The opportunity for social interaction that pupil helpers afforded was also regarded as important because peers would frequently react so as to let a pupil know when behaviour was inappropriate. Simultaneously, in the give and take of the classroom, pupils with special needs could be encouraged to be appropriately self-assertive and to use all their available skills to the maximum. This was exemplified during the observation, over a period, of a severely physically handicapped pupil who was also non-oral. In mainstream classes, a rota of volunteer pupils was assigned to this pupil in order to encourage him socially and to help him participate fully in lessons. Initially he stood out as being very different – wheelchair bound, making strange noises and dribbling profusely. Despite his odd appearance he appeared to have a sense of humour and one volunteer pupil became his particular friend. Within a few months the pupil became mobile, albeit with an awkward gait, and was encouraged and welcomed to join in class and playground games. His use of Bliss symbols as a means of communicating with his friends increased dramatically, facilitating his participation in lessons. Such anti-social behaviour as had existed, particularly over meals, ceased within weeks of joining the mainstream group for lunch. In lessons such as art and craft pupil helpers and friends were always on hand to encourage and help. Teachers remarked that he had responded to pupil help in a more positive way than he had done to adult help.

Many other instances of pupils with special needs having particular friends in class to help them with lesson content or materials were observed. Occasionally teachers expressed anxiety that pupil helpers might be giving up too much of their own class time. This was being closely monitored in one school where visually impaired pupils attended mainstream classes. One helper in particular spent considerable lesson time helping her friend, ensuring she was able to get on and had everything she needed. So far the work of the helper had not suffered, but staff believed that the increased demands expected in future examination classes would limit the amount of help she could give.

The personality of the pupil with special needs was said to be an important factor in the successful use of pupil helpers, far more so than the severity of the handicapping condition. Those pupils with unattractive personalities tended to isolate themselves from their peers and were unable to take advantage of the wealth of help and support available from their peers.

The seating arrangements for pupils with special needs often took into account the preference of helper/friend. Pupils with a sensory impairment were usually advised to sit at the front of the class, preferably with a non-handicapped friend. Sometimes a compromise was allowed if the friend did not want to sit right at the front, both pupils being allowed to sit further back.

One school with a unit for partially hearing pupils had established a unique support scheme within the main school. This scheme used volunteers from the sixth form who were willing to relinquish one or two of their free lessons a week. They were attached to a member of the partially hearing unit for certain subjects, especially the more academic subjects which involved dictated work or lengthy note taking. A large number of sixth formers had been involved with the scheme, which was in its third year. When observed, these helpers played a low key role, being very careful not to do the work for the pupil or answer questions for them. Any questions the hearing impaired pupil had about the work were directed to the class teacher. In fact, these sixth form helpers performed their task in much the same way as ancillary helpers had been seen to do in similar situations.

Pupils from the unit believed it to be of considerable help to them, many expressing the view that they felt less conspicuous talking to another, albeit older, pupil than to a teacher. Members of staff involved generally welcomed the extra help in the classroom. The sixth formers involved felt that it was a meaningful extension of their responsibilities and gave them practical experience of a minority group. A counter-argument put forward was that the sixth form helper would draw more attention to the hearing impaired in the class and cause resentment or allegations of favouritism among the hearing pupils, but in practice this did not happen, the hearing pupils readily accepting the presence of the helper as a form of support to the hearing impaired pupils.

Chapter 14
Guidelines for
Classroom Practice

This chapter seeks to offer some guidelines and teaching tips to the mainstream teacher concerned with meeting the needs of pupils in a mainstream setting. These guidelines comprise a combination of points taken from areas of good practice uncovered by project fieldwork and others cited in recent literature.

There are three sections covering the traditional categories of physical handicap, hearing impairment and visual impairment. Teaching tips to meet the needs of pupils with learning difficulties are not given separately as so much of the material available is already dealt with earlier in the book. Although the chapter is divided categorically, it will be seen that many of the points made are equally appropriate and productive across the whole area of meeting special educational needs in mainstream.

Integrating the physically handicapped pupil

This category of pupil covers a broad range of disabilities, from motor impairments (injuries and diseases of the spine, muscle, bone and joint problems), neurological impairments (cerebral palsy, muscular dystrophy, spina bifida) to other health impairments such as epilepsy, asthma, cystic fibrosis and diabetes. Cognitive functioning levels may range from profoundly retarded to gifted, and in many instances a physically handicapped pupil will display multiple handicaps (Allsop, 1980; Pasanella and Volkmor, 1981; Gearheart and Weishahn, 1980). However, it has been fairly well established that acceptability of physically handicapped pupils into the mainstream generally depends upon their being academically able (Cope and Anderson, 1977; Anderson, 1973). Despite this, recent research has shown that integration is possible and that many special educational needs can be met within the ordinary school, and indeed could be met to a far greater extent than is currently the practice. (Cope and Anderson, 1977; Hegarty and Pocklington, 1981; Hegarty, 1982). Planning is a key work in the integration of physically handicapped pupils as both physical and social factors may limit the extent to which they can join in class activities, and unnecessary hardships can be caused by lack of adequate transport or unsuitability of the school building (Spencer, 1980).

Facilitating integration

Several factors affect the pupils' acceptance by his or her peers – for instance, incontinence (when effective toileting assistance is not given), social immaturity and interrupted attendance due to repeated hospitalization (Lauder *et al.* 1978). We must remember that there are three levels of integration (physical proximity, social and academic) and that one level does not automatically lead on to the next. Total integration requires functioning at all three levels (societal integration), with the handicapped pupil becoming a naturally accepted member of the school community. Such integration requires positive attitudes and adjustments by *all* members of the school community. With physically handicapped pupils the physical environment of the classroom and school has to be even more carefully considered than modification of teaching strategies (Gearheart and Weishahn, 1980), since a majority of physically handicapped pupils accepted by mainstream schools are academically able.

a) SCHOOL ORGANIZATION
  1. As much pupil history must be accumulated as possible. Receiver staff should be able to see the pupil at home or at feeder school. This contact should alleviate many fears. Reciprocally the pupil should meet receiving staff.
  2. Staff should be aware of the ways in, and the levels at

which, the pupil communicates both verbally and in written work. Several schools in the study were able to make arrangements for the teacher in charge of pupils with special needs at the receiving ordinary school to visit pupils at work in the feeder schools, prior to their enrolment at the receiving school. The arrangement included a minimum of a day's visit to the feeder school, to observe pupils and talk with staff concerned with the pupil. In this way the teacher in charge gained first hand experience of how the pupils could cope in mainstream and through discussion with their teachers was able to gain information about materials and teaching strategies which had proved most useful. Staff felt that the information gained in this way was far more pertinent to the task of ensuring an adequate programme was provided at the receiving school than could ever be transmitted through written reports. Although such arrangements were time-consuming initially, in the long term time was saved. It ensured a smoother integration of pupils at the receiving schools, as special needs and problems were made known and acted upon prior to the pupil's arrival.

3.   In-service training is essential to acquaint staff with the handicap situation, including the most common handi-capping conditions and the psycho-physical and academic factors associated with them, and also to convince staff that beyond an unattractive body lies a real child who thinks and acts like other children (Allsop, 1980).

4.   Physical adaptations should be decided. Is it, for instance, necessary to install or arrange (a) special toileting facilities (b) ramps (c) grab rails (d) a lift (or modification in classroom usage) (e) safe storage space for crutches, etc., within reach of users? Freedom of movement, whether assisted or independent, is of greatest importance.

5.   Any special emergency procedures should be anticipated and made known to the staff concerned (Bigge and Sirvis, 1978).

6.   Help, support and advice from specialist personnel should be encouraged, for example, from specialist teachers, physio-therapists and speech therapists.

7. Class teachers should be prepared to work in the classroom with support staff such as welfare assistants and physiotherapists, and to collaborate with colleagues in order to share information and skills (Allsop, 1980; Gearheart and Weishahn, 1980; Johnson and Johnson, 1980; Schultz, 1982).

b) THE PUPIL

If physically handicapped pupils are to integrate into mainstream schooling as fully as possible, several academic and social conditions should be met.

1. The mobility of the pupil should be fully assessed: how and when physical help will be needed, what physical position and postures are to be encouraged or discouraged, what physiotherapy is necessary.

2. The physically handicapped pupil may have less energy than a non-handicapped one, thus reducing his or her ability to cope with the full school day. The class teacher needs to be alert to signs of fatigue, to provide opportunities for rest and to be prepared to reduce work volume where necessary.

3. Often, because of handicap, the pupil uses muscles with abnormal tone to perform necessary tasks. All available adaptive methods and/or aids must be used in order to increase independence and efficiency of working.

4. Teachers should be familiar with procedures for having equipment repaired when they cannot effect repairs themselves.

5. Teachers should remember that electric typewriters do not increase speed but are useful for pupils whose writing is illegible or who have limited energy.

6. A welfare helper should be available when necessary, for example, to take a pupil to the lavatory (Allsop, 1980; Gearheart and Weishahn, 1980; Johnson and Johnson, 1980; Schultz, 1982).

7. The age of the pupil should be within two years of the class average otherwise the pupil may find difficulty fitting in socially with classmates.

8. Social and emotional maturity needs to be more or less equal to that of non-handicapped classmates.

c)   THE CLASSROOM

What happens inside the classroom affects pupils' learning most immediately and it is the element of school life that is under the class teacher's control. Once a pupil enters the classroom the following points can usefully be considered.

1.   Advice on classroom management should be at hand – for instance, on the durability and suitability of certain furniture since some items are less stable (Greer and Allsop, 1978), and on adaptations to help the pupil manage books, pencils and other materials (Hoben, 1980).

2.   Suitable seating must be provided. Physically handicapped pupils must have stable, secure seating at the right height and may also need tables so that wheelchairs can get under them. Pupils can outgrow furniture and several teachers remarked on the need to monitor the arrangements.

3.   The teacher should be ready to organize the classroom to accommodate specialized equipment, such as an electric typewriter or book holders.

4.   The pupil must be allowed to be as independent as possible and it is important that the teaching space allows the pupil to move around as independently as he or she can and become an accepted social member of the group. Many staff from project schools recommended that any equipment needed by pupils is as unobtrusive as possible and does not constitute a physical barrier between handicapped pupils and their peers.

5.   If pupils have poor co-ordination the teacher should be prepared to tape paper to the desk or provide large pencils. Similarly a slant board, providing a correctly angled surface, is useful for pupils who find horizontal surfaces impossible or difficult to work on.

6.   A 'helper' or welfare assistant can be of great use in note-taking for severely handicapped pupils; extra help should only be given, however, if it is clearly needed.

7.   If writing is particularly difficult maybe a helper or a tape recorder can be used during tests.

8.   Teachers must be prepared to deal with the asthmatic, epileptic or diabetic pupil in case of emergency – to cope with a seizure, or to have sugar available for diabetics, for instance.

9. Classmates should be made familiar with the pupils' disabilities and special needs.

10. Teachers must give priority to organizing the classroom in such a way that the handicapped pupil's social and emotional development, as well as academic progress, is encouraged as much as possible.

11. Furniture should be arranged in such a way that the pupil can move freely and see all of the room in its different perspectives. This encourages incidental learning and makes the pupil feel that he or she is part of the class. Some teachers reported very good results from discussing the problem with the class. Such discussions reinforced the pupils' awareness of the need for tidiness; for instance, pushing in chairs when not in use, not leaving bags or books blocking aisles so as to allow freedom of movement for a wheelchair pupil or a pupil on crutches.

12. Crutches, wheelchairs and similar aids tend to get in the way when they are not in use. A storage area should be provided and pupils trained to keep the aids in it.

13. The handling of books may be very difficult for some physically handicapped pupils and can consume much energy. A slant board or book holder can be of great benefit; many kinds are commercially available.

14. Talking books can aid learning for pupils who are physically exhausted by traditional methods of reading.

15. Tag board or paper strips clipped to a board can be an invaluable aid as place keepers for pupils with erratic head movements. Helping the pupil to keep his or her place, or presenting material in small segments, can often make the difference between independent learning and time-consuming one-to-one tutoring.

16. Do not accept different standards of behaviour or work from handicapped pupils. They should be expected to be as clean and tidy in their workplace as their classmates. If they are mobile, with or without aids, they can be asked to run errands as often as other pupils.

17. Most physically handicapped pupils are able to take part in some form of physical education. A programme may require specialist help to begin with.

18.   Important notices must be within easy sight, perhaps placed lower than normal, particularly if the pupil is wheelchair-bound. Several teachers remarked on the degree of independence this gave pupils, enhancing their feelings of being part of the class.

19.   Physically handicapped pupils should have an equal chance to take part in the school's extra-curricular activities. Advance planning may be necessary, particularly if the pupil is taken to school by taxi. One school encouraged parents to collect pupils on the days they wished to stay later to participate in extra curricular activity. Sometimes parents are unable to do this but arrangements may be made with other parents collecting children from the same class. The fact that some pupils do have to come to school by taxi should not prevent pupils taking part in extra-curricular activities if it is at all possible for them to do so.

20.   While basic teaching methods will probably not need to be changed for physically handicapped pupils, teachers will need to be flexible as to volume (but not quality) of work and the way it is produced.

Summary

Physically handicapped pupils attending ordinary classes will need few modifications of the education programme. However, teachers and other professionals must always maintain a positive attitude and encourage a similar response in the pupil's friend and peer groups. The literature suggests that ordinary class teachers are not always prepared to work effectively with pupils who have special needs (Baum and Brazita, 1979; Middleton *et al.*, 1979; Byford, 1979; Schultz, 1982), but possibly this is because at first they do not know how to work effectively with such pupils.

From our study it would appear that once initial anxiety about having a handicapped pupil in class is overcome teachers are most concerned to ensure the full participation of these pupils in class activities. However, teacher expectations were often lower for handicapped pupils than for their non-handicapped peers.

Physically handicapped pupils are able to participate in all aspects of the curriculum although limitations may arise in physical education. Class teachers, it has been suggested, should know about the purpose, care and maintenance of general equipment such as braces, crutches and wheelchairs, but – it must be stressed – this will not be their prime responsibility. Preparation of staff is generally acknowledged to be vital and yet is often not provided (Hegarty, 1982). Insufficient staffing, including support staff or unsuitable staff deployment are other important factors which may limit an integration programme. The main conditions likely to be met by teachers in ordinary schools are given below, together with their likely effects on education.

ALLERGIES

These are fairly common and should be noted. Occasionally a pupil may miss school but allergies should not greatly interfere with his or her education.

ASTHMA

Pupils with asthma should be treated as normally as possible. Again, interference with education is unlikely.

ARTHRITIS

The educational modifications here, particularly for juvenile arthritis (Stills disease) depend on age, severity of condition, general mobility and the range of mobility in arms and fingers. Education may be interrupted if the pupil misses a considerable amount of school time during an attack or needs hospitalization.

AMPUTATION

Pupils with a prosthesis are usually able to function at nearly normal capacity and require little additional support except immediately after an operation when they are experiencing the greatest psychological effects.

DIABETES

Class teachers should be aware of insulin reactions and diabetic comas but pupils should be expected to take part in all normal school activities unless specifically restricted by a doctor.

EPILEPSY

All three common types of seizures are serious and the teacher should be aware and able to cope. Minor modifications and adjustments to the educational programme may need to be made for the pupil, particularly if the drugs used to control the epilepsy limit the pupil's learning ability.

CEREBRAL PALSY

Of the serious crippling conditions, cerebral palsy is the most common. The severity of the condition may vary considerable and a full range of educational services may be needed. The severity will dictate whether the student would best be served in a segregated or an ordinary class.

SPINA BIFIDA

These pupils usually have normal intelligence but may have multiple handicaps resulting from varying damage to the central nervous system such as varying degrees of paralysis, sensory loss, bowel and bladder incontinence and often hydrocephalus (Lauder *et al.*, 1978). Most pupils profit from ordinary class attendance with only minor modifications to the curriculum if suitable care and support are available.

MUSCULAR DYSTROPHY

During the early stages very few adjustments are necessary but as the condition progresses some modification will be essential. The pupil should be regularly reviewed and modification and support made available when necessary so that he or she is maintained in the ordinary class for as long as possible. It is to be remembered that the pupil may have to receive education at home or hospital eventually (Gearheart and Weishahn, 1980).

Integrating the hearing impaired pupil

The term *hearing impairment* includes a wide range of disability from profoundly deaf to mildly hearing impaired. The extent of the impairment may not necessarily be indicative of a pupil's ability to cope with mainstream education. That mainstream staff understand this, and the needs of hearing impaired pupils, is important particularly as present trends indicate hearing impaired pupils are increasingly being educated in mainstream schools. (Wood and Hirshoren, 1981). Thus the responsibility for their progress is going to be increasingly with the ordinary classroom teacher. It is extremely important therefore that such teachers are adequately prepared to help hearing impaired pupils participate fully in class activities.

A principal aim in the education of hearing impaired pupils is to develop the facility for the use and understanding of the spoken language so necessary for full participation in society. The question, then, is which educational environment is likely to develop this facility best: the special school, unit or ordinary class. A handicap of any sort is relative to context and it is important when considering placement for hearing impaired pupils to distinguish these constraints and limitations imposed by the handicap itself and those which may arise out of the educational environment (Lynas 1978, 1981).

If ordinary classes are considered, another important question is how far the ordinary teacher and hearing pupils should (or can) accommodate to the special needs of the hearing impaired pupil, or, conversely, how far the hearing impaired pupil can reasonably be expected to accommodate to the demands of the ordinary classroom. Certainly awareness of the implications of different teaching systems and classroom practices is important when consideration is being given to placement of the hearing impaired pupil.

Facilitating integration

To facilitate integration it seems advisable that the following conditions should be met prior to the introduction of the hearing impaired or profoundly deaf pupil to the ordinary classroom.

a) SCHOOL ORGANIZATION

1. Classroom teachers concerned should have a basic understanding of the nature of hearing impairment and its relation to learning; for example, that hearing impairment leads to delay in speech and language development and this will influence the child's ability to develop other communicative skills, of which reading is probably the most difficult. The retardation tends to be directly related to hearing loss (Jensema, 1975; Jensema and Trybus, 1978).

2. Prior to introduction to ordinary classrooms, hearing impaired pupils should have some training in developing their listening skills. Most deaf individuals have some residual hearing and the educational environment should maximize its use.

3. Classroom teachers should be a) *au fait* with hearing aids and able to check they are properly functioning b) know that the aid amplifies all sounds, therefore loud background noise can frustrate the progress of the hearing impaired pupil c) keep an extra battery/cord in the classroom.

4. Classroom teachers should be helped not to prejudge a hearing impaired pupil by being made fully aware that the severity of hearing loss is not indicative of the likely success of an integration programme.

5. Classmates should be introduced to the consequences of hearing impairment and helpful techniques facilitating communication. In many schools visited it was reported that classmates had quickly become 'masters' at communicating with their hearing impaired peers and could provide valuable help to the class teacher in this respect.

b) THE PUPIL

There are several academic and social qualities which should be optimally possessed by hearing impaired pupils for whom normal schooling is being considered.

1. The pupil is able to use any residual hearing and can cope with full-time hearing aid usage.

2. The pupils' language and speech skills are not too significantly below those of the class groups.

3. The pupil's age is within two years of class average, otherwise he may find difficulty in fitting in with classmates.
4. The social/emotional maturity is equal, or nearly equal, to that of hearing classmates.
5. The pupil is sufficiently self-confident, independent and determined to function in the normal class.
6. The ability and concentration of hearing impaired pupils are within the range for the proposed class.

(from Griffin, 1970 and Northcott, 1973)

It has been shown that the closer the hearing impaired child's academic abilities are to those of his peers, the greater the chances for academic success in integration, and that the amount of hearing loss is not a reliable pointer to success here (Gonzales, 1980).

c) THE CLASSROOM

Once in the classroom the following guidelines will help the hearing impaired pupil function to his/her maximum potential.

1. Find the best seating arrangement for the hearing impaired pupil where he or she can hear/lipread best. Some experimentation may be necessary, remembering that it becomes difficult to lipread beyond 8–10 feet.

In some situations, for example, classroom discussions, the hearing impaired pupil is naturally at a disadvantage. In such situations the hearing impaired pupil is unable to predict the next speaker and will lose valuable visual cues whilst trying to locate him/her. It is often during such exchanges that the hearing impaired pupil becomes 'lost', may withdraw from the situation mentally or become disruptive in an effort to control the situation. Hearing impaired pupils should be allowed to move to a position where they can best observe all their peers and, with some teacher control of the discussion, may be able to pick up some of the points. It has to be remembered, however, that class discussions always put the hearing impaired pupil to a great disadvantage. Class discussions are nevertheless an important part of class activities and should not be abandoned because of the presence of a hearing impaired pupil. Simply summarizing the major points of the discussion at the end can provide the hearing impaired pupil with an adequate alternative.

2. Teacher/peer speech should be normal and the speech rate moderate. Exaggerated mouth movements and incomplete sentences can be misleading.

3. To facilitate lipreading speakers should always face the hearing impaired pupil, and avoid standing with their backs to a window or light source. The light source should always be behind the hearing impaired pupil.

4. Gestures, if used, should be natural, not exaggerated, as excessive movement can be distracting.

5. Of the many technical aids available to the classroom teacher, only a few will be of benefit to the hearing impaired pupil, e.g. use of the overhead projector can be of enormous benefit as the teacher can face the class whilst the projected slides are on view. Later the slides could be made available to the hearing impaired pupil, to copy. However, material presented on tape, audio cassette and much material on video may be difficult, if not impossible for the pupil to follow.

6. It is helpful when teaching to use as many visual cues as possible, e.g. pointing to objects or diagrams being spoken about. 'Those who cannot hear must use eyes instead of ears to receive information and in this respect are very different from hearing persons.' (Stokoe, 1976)

Although adapting a teaching style may be necessary to maintain progress, suggested alterations must not be understood to imply criticism of the way a teacher works but simply that as a hearing person the teacher may not be wholly aware of all the difficulties a hearing impaired pupil has in normal, everyday situations. In presenting material care must be taken to use language consistent with the material taught, not to be overly complex or go too quickly through the material. Indeed, we observed that it was often helpful to other pupils as well as the hearing impaired pupil for the teacher to paraphrase, simplify and repeat those points critical to the concept being taught.

Use of visual aids such as written instructions and summaries is extremely important, and when combined with good oral presentation and periodic verification should be enough to enable the hearing impaired pupil to follow the main thrust of the lesson. It is indicative that there is lack of understanding if a hearing impaired pupil who normally tries hard starts to withdraw or becomes difficult. The pupil must be encouraged to ask questions, but from our observations this is something that hearing impaired pupils are very reluctant to do.

7. It is almost impossible for a hearing impaired pupil to look at material, e.g. maps and books, and simultaneously listen to what the teacher is saying. Wherever possible, such teaching styles should be modified to take into account the hearing impaired pupil, and where such techniques may be necessary, for example, map reading, it may be possible to use a 'friend' to provide special help as necessary. The 'friend' could be a classmate or welfare help.

8. A hearing impaired pupil has difficulty localizing sound and would therefore experience difficulty following a questions and answers session around the class. Such a problem is overcome if the teacher repeats such questions and answers.

9. It is not advisable to assume that the hearing impaired pupil is getting the same information from a class as his normal hearing peers (Hedgecock 1974). Thus it is helpful to summarize lesson points on the blackboard and to put up key words and homework. Also, if possible it is most helpful to the hearing impaired pupil to have lesson notes to take away at the end of each session.

10. Class teachers should watch out for signs of fatigue, remembering that lipreading is extremely tiring over long periods. The pupil may not always pay attention. It is important to determine why a pupil is not paying attention, and there are a number of possibilities to be investigated. The aid itself may not be working efficiently or the ambient noise may be too high; in some areas there may have been insufficient back-up support given or the pupil may simply be tired. The latter point is particularly critical, as trying to comprehend verbal messages all day with an imperfect linguistic and auditory system is extremely tiring and by early afternoon many hearing impaired pupils are unable to cope. It would be desirable if as many of the language based subjects

as possible could be scheduled for the morning, although with complex timetabling considerations this may not always be possible at secondary level. If it is impossible to reschedule lessons, class teachers may have to be made aware that hearing impaired pupils may not function fully in the afternoons and may require more help than usual in class to maintain progress.

11. Co-operative working arrangements with the specialist teacher of the deaf and the classroom teacher can greatly aid integration. Such arrangements may include a specialist teacher modifying or adapting class materials, giving back-up support at the end of a topic or prior to the introduction of a new topic (remembering most deaf pupils do not read as well as their peers) (Culhane and Curwin, 1978).

12. The class teacher should make sure of the hearing impaired pupil's attention before speaking – a 'helper' may be of use here.

13. It must be remembered that it is not unlikely that a hearing impaired pupil will require supportive assistance throughout his or her school career (see Gearheart and Weishahn 1980, Pasanella and Volkmor 1981).

14. It is most useful to observe the hearing impaired pupil in unstructured situations, for example, breaks and lunchtimes, to ascertain the status of the pupil within the peer group, and whether or not the pupil is a full participant in the group's activities. Acceptance within the peer group has a direct and important bearing on the pupil's education, as an unhappy, isolated pupil is unlikely to be fully receptive to mainstream teaching. Once aware of the situation, the class teacher may be able to help the pupil improve his or her status within the group if this proves necessary.

Summary

To maximize a hearing impaired pupil's potential to integrate, all the above points must be taken into account adequately. To expect the classroom teacher to cope without some form of in-service training may hinder the process of integration. Such training would give the teachers the knowledge and information necessary to understand the educational problems of hearing impaired pupils and the confidence to begin to cope with them. Our observations in schools suggest that the hearing impaired pupil is expected to follow the curriculum for the mainstream class. He or she should be able to perform adequately within the group if the placement is correct and if he or she receives extra assistance to enable progress to be maintained. One very effective programme observed was the preview, teach and review paradigm, in which the specialist teacher previewed prospective lessons by discussing content, new concepts and language. The class teacher then presented the lesson (the 'teach' component) after which the specialist teacher reviewed the material to ensure understanding. Such support was not needed in all subject areas, but the indications were that support would be necessary for some subjects and would be needed throughout the pupil's school career. Continued support throughout this career is likely to be necessary because hearing is unlikely to improve, and thus the pupil will continue to miss auditory/verbal material.

Integrating visually impaired pupils

The term 'visual impairment' can cover a variety of conditions ranging from the need to wear corrective spectacles to blindness, but is usually limited to those children referred to as 'partially sighted' or 'blind'. Sometimes a child is categorized according to the mode of reading, as, for example, a 'braille' reader or 'print' reader, which is possibly more applicable to educationalists; but this can be deceptive as it depends on teacher preference and skill, availability of low vision aids and so on (Reynold and Birch, 1977).

From an educational point of view it is as well to bear in mind that visual acuity may vary at different times and under different circumstances, fatigue, illness or levels of lighting, for example. The majority of pupils registered blind do in fact have some residual vision which they should be encouraged to use as it will rarely be harmed by use, but may deteriorate through lack of use.

The visual impairment may be such that the child can cope with reading print at very close range, but not with moving freely round his environment. Therefore the education programme must be tailored to meet the pupil's total developmental needs including those resulting from the visual impairment.

Facilitating integration

When a visually impaired pupil is to be admitted to mainstream school or class a number of preparations can be made which effect a reduction in teacher/pupil anxiety and help the proposed programme to run smoothly.

a) SCHOOL ORGANIZATION
  1. It is useful to have collated as much information about the pupil as possible. Discussions with medical staff, teachers parents and former teachers can be very helpful in this respect.
  2. If the pupil is a print reader, it may be necessary to locate a source of large print materials, which can take considerable time, a factor often overlooked in lesson planning.
  3. The pupil may require special adaptive aids or need special equipment (an optacon, for example) to make full use of print materials, and these should be made available.
  4. If the pupil is to have back-up support from a specialist teacher, arrangements should be made with the specialist services for the teacher to be available at the start of the programme. Much unnecessary hardship to pupil and class teacher alike was reported when such specialist help was unavailable at the start of a programme.
  5. If the pupil is a braille reader, a source of such materials must be located as well as any other specialist equivalent such as a braille typewriter, talking calculator and tape recorders.
  6. Good illumination is an important factor which enables a pupil to make optimal use of residual vision. If lighting levels are deficient a simple remedy may be the acquisition of a portable reading lamp for close work.
  7. Visually impaired pupils can often cope with board work if this is a white board, and it can be helpful if the school has installed these in preference to blackboards.
  8. Mainstream staff should be familiarized with the abilities and limitations of the visually impaired pupil.

b) THE PUPIL
There are several academic and social qualities which should be optimally possessed by visually impaired pupils for whom mainstream schooling is being considered.
 1. If the pupil has residual vision it is useful if he or she is trained and encouraged to use it and can cope with special adaptive aids.
 2. The age of the pupil should be within two years of the class average, otherwise there may be difficulty in the pupil being accepted socially by classmates.
 3. The social/emotional maturity should be equal, or nearly equal, to that of seeing classmates.
 4. The ability and concentration of the visually impaired pupil should be within the range for the proposed class.
 5. Opportunities to familiarize the pupil with the classroom and school design should be arranged.

c) THE CLASSROOM
On entry to the classroom it is helpful if the following points are given consideration.
 1. Orientation of the pupil should continue. It is helpful if the pupil practises walking in and round the playground, dining area and classroom. These sessions may involve 'helpers' and can also be used as 'getting acquainted' sessions.
 2. For the pupil with partial sight, placement within the class is crucial to success. Viewing distance and the degree of illumination required must be carefully considered.
 3. As for hearing impaired pupils, situations which produce a glare – for example, standing with the light source behind the teacher – are to be avoided.
 4. If special materials and equipment are to be used, a check should be made to ensure that these are being properly used.
 5. It is helpful if handouts are in black ink and transcribed into large size if necessary (a student helper or welfare assistant could do this).
 6. The teacher should verbalize anything written on the board (preferably this should be white, using black felt pens). Blue ink can be difficult to see.
 7. The visually impaired pupil should be given every

opportunity to use his or her other senses to learn. The teacher should, therefore, provide concrete learning materials wherever possible. 'If a child cannot see materials well enough to learn the intended concepts or skills, provide suitable tactile or auditory materials to teach these things' (Von Hippel 1977). It must be remembered that some materials can be unpleasant to touch or smell, therefore careful introduction of materials is essential to avoid problems.

8. Any physical changes in the room should be explained to the students, and noise levels should be kept as low as possible as visually impaired students make frequent use of auditory cues.

9. When giving directions to a specific destination it is important to make the directions non-visual (use compass and right and left cues) and to give them from the point at which the pupil is.

10. When describing the location of an object on a flat surface, a desk, for example, teachers should use clock directions: e.g. the rubber is at 2 o'clock.

11. Teachers should use the sighted-guide technique to help blind pupils through new areas. (Points 9, 10 and 11 should be explained to classmates.)

12. Doors should not be left ajar. (Have them either always open or always closed.)

13. The teacher should not accept different standards of behaviour for visually impaired pupils. The visually impaired pupil should be expected to clean up his or her working area, and when proficient in travelling around the school he or she can be called on to run errands as often as other children.

14. Sometimes visually impaired pupils develop unusual mannerisms and they must be reminded (gently) about more appropriate behaviours. Again it was found that the best tutors in this respect seemed to be classmates.

15. All visually impaired pupils should take part in PE lessons as they generally have little opportunity or motivation to bend, stretch, run, tumble, skip etc. The programme may necessitate specialist help to begin with.

16. As with social behaviour, the curriculum and standards of work should not be different for the visually impaired pupil (except maybe substitution of some materials).

17. When speaking to a visually impaired student the teacher should use his/her name first to ensure attention.

18. The teacher should always talk directly to the pupil, looking him or her in the face (teachers should remind classmates of this).

19. The pupil must be told who is speaking to him or her when approached, and must be told when the speaker is going.

20. It is best to use speech that contains words related to sight, e.g. 'see', 'look', as visually impaired pupils use these words anyway.

21. The teacher should encourage the pupil to ask for assistance when required, and should not assist before the pupil is asked if he or she would like help.

22. The pupil should be encouraged to use his/her aids.

23. If necessary, a book stand could be provided which will bring the work closer to the pupil's eyes, thus avoiding fatigue.

24. Noticeboards should be within arm's length, particularly if notices in braille or large print notices are to be placed on them.

25. Specialist teachers are available, and often a visually impaired pupil will be supported by a specialist teacher. The class teacher should use every opportunity to take advantage of this specialist knowledge. Obviously this will probably require advanced planning and good communication.

26. Equal opportunities should be made available for visually impaired pupils to participate in the extra-curricular activities of the school. Again this will possibly require advanced planning particularly if the pupil is taxied to school.

27. As visually impaired pupils cannot see how their peers are tackling a problem, they need particularly clear instructions from class teachers.

d) PLANNING A PROGRAMME FOR THE VISUALLY IMPAIRED

If sensory information is limited, the result can be delay in cognitive and motor development so there is a call for an educational programme providing concrete practical experience and ordered stimulation (Harley, 1963 and Lowenfield, 1973).

However, it has been found that many blind pupils can learn to function well in the ordinary classroom situation if back-up support is available from specialist teachers, but most partially sighted pupils can integrate fully without the need for specialist teacher help. The child who is visually impaired is going to be limited in his or her ability to learn through conventional means (mainly visual in the normal population), so must be given opportunities to develop mobility, spatial orientation, concept and social develop ment (Cutsforth, 1951, Cratty and Sams, 1968, Cratty, 1971, Lowenfield, 1973, and Reynolds and Birch, 1977). Concept development may be restricted and is often dependent on input from the other senses. The quantity of sensory input may be restricted because some parts of the environment are inaccessible, for example sky or hills, or there is a lack of opportunity to explore that which could be made accessible. Verbal learning, not having appropriate foundation in concrete experience, can create problems for visually impaired pupils' learning. The visually impaired, particularly if severely impaired, are at a disadvantage in observing objects as a whole and relating these objects to the environment.

Alternative teaching strategies for visually impaired pupils do not generally involve a significant change in the normal teaching strategies of the class teacher. However, instruction should always be initiated at the concrete level (i.e. learning by doing) (Barraga, 1970, 76). The pupil who cannot see invariably gains less from visual stimulation, and if a large part of lesson time is geared to charts, maps or board work, that pupil may become frustrated as he or she cannot do the same work as the rest of the class, feels isolated and slips into a dream world or develops attention-seeking behaviour which may become disruptive. Thus mainstream staff should be encouraged to emphasize material in an auditory and tactile mode as well as in the visual mode.

What is very important to take into account in planning an education programme is the age of onset and the manner in which it occurred. The former has a major impact on development, functioning and learning. A child will lack colour concepts and often be unable to draw on visual imagery if there was severe loss of vision prior to age 5–7 years. (Schlaegel, 1953, and Blank, 1958). Obviously with sudden onset of visual loss there may be greater psychological adjustments then with a less rapid onset (Cutsforth, 1951, Lavenfield, 1973).

It may be necessary to extend the time allowed to a visually impaired pupil when working or doing a test, as reading or writing takes longer for the visually impaired. Braille writing is usually interpreted for class teachers by the specialist, but every encouragement should be given to the visually impaired pupil to use any residual sight. From an educational point of view it is as well to bear in mind that visual acuity may vary at different times and under different circumstances, e.g. during periods of fatigue or illness, or with different levels of lighting.

The visual impairment may be such that the child can cope with reading print at very close range but not with moving freely round his environment. Therefore the education programme must be tailored to meet the pupil's total developmental needs, including those resulting from the visual impairment.

Visually impaired pupils will sometimes go to great lengths to conceal their difficulties from teachers and classmates. Some pupils we observed did not discuss difficulties with reading from the board or poorly duplicated sheets with staff but preferred instead to rely on their neighbours for help. Often incorrect copying led to problems with lesson content and understanding of concepts not immediately apparent without close observation and questioning by the teacher. It is advisable for teachers to bear in mind that using residual vision, although recommended, may be very fatiguing if close work is done throughout the day, and by early afternoon many visually impaired pupils are unable to cope fully. If possible, the timetable should allow breaks between periods of close work activities to allow the ciliary muscles to recover.

Summary

From our observations in schools, we conclude that the visually impaired pupil is expected to follow the curriculum for that class. Indeed, the visually impaired pupil should be able to perform adequately within the group if the placement is correct and if he or she receives extra assistance to enable progress to be maintained. Communication and co-operation between the specialist and class teacher is to be emphasized and following such, the visually impaired pupils can be easily accommodated to integrate into mainstream. It is also to be emphasized that back-up support and training for the ordinary class teacher is of considerable importance. Indeed it has been stated that for such integration programmes 'extensive preparation is vital to success' (Simon and Gillman, 1979), a view supported by our researches.

Chapter 15
Summary

Teaching pupils with special needs is not a totally different enterprise from teaching other pupils. It represents a considerable challenge nevertheless to many ordinary schools and to many teachers who had never anticipated teaching such pupils. Apart from the fact that it is commonly perceived as something new and difficult, it requires changes at two levels: the academic organization and curricular provision of the school, and the professional development of individual teachers.

This study has focused on these changes, not from a theoretical or speculative viewpoint but from the practical perspective of scrutinizing existing practice. It is perfectly possible to say what schools and teachers need to do in principle in order to accommodate pupils with special needs. It is quite another matter to develop realistic strategies for change which are based on and grow out of existing classroom practice.

In seeking to do the latter we accepted a constraint which limited our enquiry but which may also be seen as adding to the strength of the findings. With the exception of Chapter 14 the book is based entirely on observed practice in schools in England and Wales. None of the practice described is too far removed from what is possible in the majority of schools. We would note also that the book is based on observations in and information obtained from some seventy schools. We made extensive enquiries and consulted widely in developing our sample and, while we will have missed some examples of innovative practice, it is reasonable to claim that it was a fair cross-section of current efforts to accommodate pupils with special needs in the mainstream.

Academic organization

An initial consideration is the academic organization of the school. We have looked at this in terms of how pupils are grouped for teaching purposes and how supplementary teaching outside mainstream lessons is organized for those who need it. Cutting across these factors and imposing its own constraints is the further matter of timetabling.

Pupils are grouped for teaching purposes in a great variety of ways in British schools, particularly at secondary level. Arrangements for pupils with special needs must be seen in the light of how the school as a whole is structured. Mixed ability classes, for instance, were widely perceived as advantageous in offering the flexibility of teaching approach necessary for these pupils. There were some clear limits, however. It was found helpful if no more than two pupils with special needs were allocated to any one class since the demands on the teacher were otherwise too great. Also, two pupils with similar special needs could be accommodated more easily than two pupils with very different educational needs. Other factors to take into account were the ethos and academic standard of the receiving class, the personality of the pupil and correspondingly the personality and attitudes of the receiving teacher, the nature of the subject and the pupil's special needs.

Pupils with special needs were absorbed into the academic life of schools in numerous ways. The diversity of organization of patterns can be described in terms of a loose continuum.

  i) Mainstream placement with extra educational support provided for individual pupils. An improved pupil/teacher ratio in the school as a whole.

 ii) Mainstream placement with pupil support for specific curricular areas. Care support as necessary. Teacher appointed with specific responsibility for pupils with special educational needs.

iii) Mainstream placement and withdrawal for specialist teaching to a resource area or to peripatetic staff. Care support as necessary.

 iv) Mainstream base, attending special unit part-time for 'on site' specialist teaching. Care support as necessary.

v) Unit/special class base and mainstream classes part-time. Care support as necessary.
vi) Unit/special class base throughout. Care support as necessary.
vii) Mainstream school as base and special school part-time.
viii) Special school as base and mainstream school part-time.

These patterns are not totally separate from each other. They overlap in practice, and provision in a given school can comprise elements of several different patterns. Caution should be exercised too in viewing the listing as a continuum. Depending on what facet of the provision is in focus – amount of individual teaching support, time spent with peers, departure from mainstream school organization – it could be placed at different points along the continum. For example, a pupil who is based in the mainstream might spend the greater part of the day withdrawn for specialist teaching, while another who is based in a unit could well be attending a majority of mainstream lessons. What the listing does provide is a convenient way of categorizing the diversity of organizational arrangements that schools make to accommodate pupils with special needs. This in turn facilitates the exploration of the implications of different forms of provision for both pupil and teacher.

Related to pupil grouping but independent of it were the arrangements school made for supplementary teaching outside mainstream lessons. This was provided before, during and after lessons.

1. Pre-lesson teaching

Some pupils were prepared for mainstream lessons by means of specific instruction given beforehand, generally on an individual basis. This could take the form of introducing new concepts and topics of work before they arose in mainstream lessons, explaining potentially difficult vocabulary or rehearsing expressive and interpersonal skills such as might be required in drama lessons.

For this tuition to be effective teachers needed to know what was being planned for the mainstream lesson(s). This placed a high premium on liaison and the exchange of information. Where liaison was well established, the support teacher obtained adequate advance knowledge – on a weekly, monthly or even half termly basis – of the content to be covered along with copies of resource materials as appropriate, while the class teacher became informed on the difficulties (with this learning material) that might be anticipated for a given pupil and what preparatory groundwork was being carried out. The major difficulty in practice was finding time for this liaison. A timetabled meeting for the exchange of information was rarely possible. Staff generally liaised informally when it was mutually convenient, though meetings at lunchtime and at the end of the day were held in some schools.

2.   *Supplementary teaching provided during a mainstream lesson*

When supplementary teaching was provided during a mainstream lesson this usually took place within the classroom, whether through team teaching or the use of a second adult in some way. In a few cases, however, particularly where pupils with a sensory impairment were concerned, this teaching was provided outside the classroom. Thus, a partially sighted pupil watching a television programme might need frequent explanations in the course of the programme in order to make sense of it. If this is done within the classroom, it can be intrusive for other pupils and can also single out the pupil in an unwelcome way. As with pre-lesson teaching, there is need of regular liaison between the person responsible for the withdrawal and the class teacher.

The ways in which pupils were withdrawn from lessons and the purposes this served differed as between primary and secondary sectors. Younger pupils were withdrawn for short periods – often lasting for part of a lesson only – when teachers deemed this to be necessary. As a rule they used different resource materials at these times, but concepts were reinforced and skills developed which were related to current work in the classroom and geared to the pupil's level of development – all under the control of a teacher or classroom assistant. At secondary level, by contrast, it was common for pupils to take the initiative in leaving the classroom themselves. This was often to use specialist equipment such as closed circuit television or recording equipment. They were expected to decide for themselves when they should leave the classroom in this way. Since this was rarely for specific teaching purposes, supervision rather than additional teaching was required.

3. *Post-lesson teaching*

The most common form of supplementary teaching was that which came after lessons. This served the dual function of monitoring pupils' progress and dealing with any difficulties arising. It has to be timetabled to occur as soon as possible after a lesson but so as not to prevent a pupil from attending other important lessons. (This latter imposed a clear restriction on the amount of support teaching that could be provided in this way.)

Support was usually provided by a specialist teacher (or classroom assistant), i.e. not the class teacher, so that there was need of information on the content of the lesson and the material used in it. When lack of time or organization prevented the exchange of information between teachers, support teachers relied heavily on pupils themselves to fill them in on class work as well as the difficulties they had experienced. A common pattern was to discuss the mainstream lesson, checking through what had been covered, reviewing concepts and their application, reinforcing vocabulary and generally ensuring that the content of the lesson was properly understood. A particular advantage of back-up teaching time was that it gave pupils easier opportunity to ask questions. Many pupils with special needs hesitated to ask questions which might display their lack of knowledge in the mainstream lesson and so lost the chance both to check their grasp of the topic and to participate actively in the lesson. Encouraging them to ask questions and discuss topics not only enhanced their understanding but in some cases increased pupils' confidence to a point where they could play a more active part in mainstream lessons.

4. *Pre- and post-lesson support*

In a small number of schools the effort was made to provide support before *and* after mainstream lessons in an integrated way. This was expensive in terms of staff time, both in providing such a high level of additional support and engaging in the consultation and plannning that it demanded. For this reason its use was generally confined to secondary schools, where pupils were following a subject-based curriculum, and especially when learning was perceived to be sequential in nature.

Timetabling is a further aspect of academic organization that has particular relevance to pupils with special needs. To the extent that many of them follow individual programmes, dividing their time between mainstream lessons and a unit base or withdrawal arrangements, care has to be taken in drawing up programmes of work to ensure that they slot in with the mainstream timetable and that the programmes are not distorted by timetabling constraints. Back-up teaching must be incorporated into timetable planning so that teacher availability can be matched with pupil requirement.

The involvement of external agencies introduced further considerations. When a school has links with a special school, some dovetailing of the daily timetable may well be necessary. Visits from peripatetic teachers and speech and physiotherapists are of most benefit if they can be anticipated and related to pupils' other work in an appropriate way. Indeed, when this does not happen and visiting professionals arrive at inconvenient times it can disrupt a pupil's programme.

Constructing a timetable can be a complicated exercise, particularly in large secondary schools with multiple curricular options, and the presence of pupils with special needs has the effect of complicating it further. If a school is to be serious about teaching these pupils in a mainstream setting, however, it has to accept this complication. Information on pupils' teaching and curriculum requirements must be assembled at an early stage and incorporated into the school's timetable as an integral part of it when it is first drawn up.

Modification to curriculum content

If pupils with special needs are to be educated adequately in mainstream schools there is need of considerable curriculum development. In general terms, these pupils have been excluded from the mainstream because of the absence of suitable educational provision for them. Consequently mainstream schools are faced with the task of modifying their curricula and ensuring that these pupils engage in learning activities appropriate to their needs. The content of the curriculum varied greatly in the schools studied. This variety can be described in terms of a continuum running parallel to that used in describing schools' organizational patterns. With a notional mainstream curriculum followed by the main pupil body at one end and a totally segregated curriculum for pupils with severe and complex needs at the other, this continuum can be outlined in terms of five points:

  i) Mainstream curriculum
 ii) Mainstream curriculum with some modification
iii) Mainstream curriculum with significant modification
 iv) Special curriculum with additions
  v) Special curriculum.

i) *Mainstream curriculum*

When pupils were doing the same work in the same teaching groups as peers they were effectively following a mainstream currciulum. Some schools sought to restrict their intake of pupils with special needs to those who could cope intellectually with the existing mainstream curriculum. As might be expected, the pupils concerned were usually either physically handicapped or visually impaired. Efforts might be made, by modifying the teaching approach, to enhance access to the content, but the content itself was not changed.

ii)   *Mainstream curriculum with some modification*

Some pupils with sensory impairment followed essentially the
same curriculum as their peers apart from modifications related
directly to their impairment. Thus some visually impaired pupils
learned typing or braille, physically handicapped pupils
developed skills which compensated for specific motor deficiencies and hearing impaired pupils engaged in extra work on
language. Staff sought to incorporate these modifications with as
little disruption as possible, but inevitably there were cases when
alternative or supplementary activities were only possible at the
expense of some area of the mainstream curriculum. Foreign
language teaching, especially for hearing impaired pupils, was a
regular casualty in this context.

iii)   *Mainstream curriculum with significant modification*

The emphasis here was still on making available as much of the
mainstream curriculum as possible but taking greater account of
pupils' individual needs and capacities. This entailed modifying
the mainstream curriculum to a greater or lesser extent, usually
in the context of a unit base or a significant amount of
withdrawal from mainstream lessons. These arrangements were
usually made in favour of pupils with moderate learning
difficulties or those with severe hearing losses.

   The most common pattern was to supplement mainstream
English and maths with additional work on a withdrawal basis
or, alternatively, to provide language and number work on an
entirely separate basis. Other subjects were taken as part of a
mainstream group though with considerable variation in practice from school to school. Depending on how much additional
time was given over to literacy and numeracy, some subjects
were dropped or given less time and attention.

iv)   *Special curriculum with additions*

The emphasis here was on pupils' special needs and, while the
curriculum might cover a range of educational experiences, its

primary definition was in terms of how these pupils were different from their peers rather than what they had in common with them. The starting point in curriculum development was individual needs, and only when these were seen to be met was consideration given to the parts of the mainstream curriculum that could then be made available. In operational terms this resulted in a heavy concentration on basic work in language and number, with extension into other curricular areas having secondary importance.

v) *Special curriculum*

Pupils with severe and complex learning difficulties were sometimes offered a curriculum that had little or no reference to work done in the mainstream. As such it has no relevance to integration. Such curricula tended to be based on precisely defined objectives, covering basic communication and social skills within a developmental framework.

Staffing

Educating pupils with special needs in the mainstream has major implications for school staff. This can be seen at various levels: staffing establishments, for both ancillaries and teachers, must be revised; attitudes may have to change; individuals' roles need to evolve; channels for transmitting information must be set up; and above all, perhaps, staff should have access to in-service opportunities in order to further relevant professional development.

An important staffing initiative in many of the schools studied was the setting up of a post with specific responsibility for all pupils with special needs in the school. The role of this designated teacher was typically multi-faceted, combining some or all of the following: teaching pupils with special needs; monitoring such pupils' progress; devising individual programmes or work; supporting mainstream teachers, both inside and outside the classroom; teaching mainstream classes; disseminating information; taking responsibility for in-service work; liaising with external agencies; administration. The wide-ranging responsibilities given to these teachers highlights the importance of their role. It was found too that their liaising and coordinating functions were facilitated by appointing them at a relatively senior level within the school.

Another important area of development was the deployment of ancillary staff. Teachers identified ancillary staff as a major resource in educating pupils with special needs. Apart from attending to care needs, which was often the initial reason for employing them, they could provide a level of support that freed teachers to concentrate on teaching and reduced demands of a non-teaching nature on teacher time. In some schools ancillary staff were given a more specifically educational role, either working with one or more pupils under the teacher's instructions or implementing a programme drawn up by a visiting speech or physiotherapist.

Acquiring relevant information about the pupils they taught was a major issue with the mainstream teachers interviewed. Where information was available it tended to come through one of four routes: lists, possibly annotated; pupil files; staff meetings; and direct contact with either peripatetic staff or a designated teacher within the school. The last of these was considered to work well when invoked. In general, however, teachers felt that they lacked information on pupils' handicapping conditions and on the implications for teaching that arose from them.

The professional development of teachers which is such a necessary part of integration was pursued in two ways by schools in our study: school-based courses and professional contact. In a number of cases the stimulus for in-service work came from internal discussions about staff needs and development. This led to a school drawing up and implementing its own in-service course. Content and approach naturally varied according to the type of school and the special educational needs that were uppermost in people's minds. Most courses comprised between ten and fifteen lectures/workshops, drawing on professionals from the community as well as any specialist staff in post. Additional elements in some courses were visits, extended staff discussion and residential weekends.

Contact with specialist staff was a further, if somewhat

spasmodic, form of professional development. Mainstream teachers could acquire a good deal of useful information and knowledge through contact with expert colleagues – on-site specialist teachers, peripatetic teachers, psychologists and others. A bonus was that this information was practically based and related to a pupil that the teacher was currently dealing with. On the negative side, this contact was difficult to establish and tended to be irregular, so that any knowledge teachers picked up was patchy and confined to a narrow context.

Teaching

What matters in the end is how pupils are taught, whether in the classroom alongside peers or withdrawn from it for individual or small group tuition. So we looked at classroom organization, how teachers presented subject matter and interacted with pupils to facilitate learning, arrangements for monitoring pupils' progress, and the use of second adults and pupil helpers in the classroom. Finally, we present guidelines drawn from the literature as well as from our fieldwork that are relevant to the teaching and classroom management of different categories of pupils with special needs.

Classroom organization is used here in the sense of physical layout and four aspects of it are considered: arrangement of furniture; seating and grouping of pupils; acoustics; and lighting. The arrangement of furniture has most obvious relevance to pupils with physical handicaps. If mobility is restricted, thought must be given to permitting access to different parts of the room (if pupils are expected to move about during lessons) and to areas of escape in case of fire. This was easier to achieve in large rooms and in open plan teaching areas than in classrooms where the traditional arrangement of desks in rows separated by narrow aisles obtained. It was of course easier for teachers to rearrange furniture by blocking, creating double aisles and so on when they had exclusive use of the room – a situation more likely to obtain at primary level. Some rearrangement can be beneficial also for pupils other than the physically handicapped; thus pupils with impaired hearing can participate more easily in class discussion if desks are arranged in a semi-circle. Additional requirements are space for specialist equipment and work tables, corresponding storage space and access to power points.

Teachers need to ensure that pupils with special needs are seated in the most suitable position for them to maximize their learning and to participate as fully as possible in all classroom activities. This may mean different things to different pupils. Those with impaired hearing should be able to see the faces of speakers without any blurring background lights. Partially sighted pupils are generally best seated toward the front and should be free to move up close to the blackboard or projector screen as necessary. Pupils with severe visual handicap need of course to be warned of changes in classroom layout and should be protected from clutter such as bags left in aisles or passageways. When pupils are supported in the classroom by an extra teacher or ancillary it was usually found least intrusive if they were seated at the back of the room or toward one side.

Acoustics and lighting have particular relevance to pupils with hearing and visual impairment respectively. In many classrooms a level of working noise is tolerated which can present problems for some partially hearing pupils. Physical modifications to improve acoustic insulation and damping can help but teachers generally found that most improvement came from changing the way they managed the classroom. As regards lighting, there were two main considerations: providing high levels of illumination for those who needed it, and ensuring that pupils benefited as much as possible from common display material. The former necessitated individual desk lamps, often only possible through the use of lengthy – and potentially dangerous – extension leads. The latter required such steps as regular maintenance of artificial lighting sources, minimizing glare and reflection through use of matt surfaces and having proper blackout when films and slides were shown.

Teachers' classroom practice can be considered under three headings: preparing subject material; presenting it to pupils; and interacting with pupils to facilitate their learning. An initial task in preparing material was to identify the key concepts which had to be covered if pupils were to cope with topic areas. Many teachers prepared handouts incorporating basic concepts and information, presented in a direct and simple way. Workcards and general handouts for the class were sometimes adapted for pupils with learning difficulties, or accompanied by an additional sheet which gave simple explanations of key terms. Some teachers paid particular attention to preparing for experimental work, providing pupils with a list of everything needed for the experiment, step-by-step descriptions of how to perform them and detailed guidelines to structure the writing up. A further level of preparation was necessary for visually impaired pupils who required enlarged print or braille materials; these had to be ordered well in advance and required teachers to plan the content of their lesson well ahead of time.

The presentation of learning material to a group of pupils follows on from how it has been prepared. Where pupils had difficulties in learning teachers found it advantageous to introduce topics in a slow step-by-step way, using concrete examples and objects wherever possible. Frequent repetition gauged by feedback from the pupils was also necessary. Topics with a direct reference to a specific sensory input may require a different mode of presentation for pupils with the corresponding sensory impairment. Thus, topics such as reflection or shadow might be exemplified using heat lamps instead of light sources for visually impaired pupils. As an aside, it may be noted that teachers' efforts to rethink their mode of presentation for the sake of pupils with special needs benefited many other pupils as well; their learning and grasp of topics were enhanced by a presentation style that was pedagogically better structured and was more sensitive to pupil feedback.

A particular problem of presentation arises when pupils with learning difficulties are being taught in mixed ability lessons. The degree of repetition and simplification of instructions necessary for the sake of one or two pupils may be counterproductive for the rest of the class. Some teachers coped with this situation by engaging in a modified presentation to those pupils that needed it immediately after whole class instruction. Others found it helpful to break the class into groups of four or five; explanations and instructions given to the class as a whole were repeated and clarified within the groups for the sake of those who had difficulties with them. This was found to work particularly well when the group was engaged on a project or other common task.

Teacher interaction with pupils to facilitate their learning is a

major component of the teaching process. This entails asking
questions, promoting discussion and generally engaging in
verbal interaction. We examined this in terms of the frequency
with which such interaction took place, the comprehensibility of
the language used and the nature of any reinforcement given.
The amount and frequency of interaction between teachers
and pupils with special needs varied widely, not always in
accordance with the latter's need of it. Many pupils with special
needs benefited from more instructional time than their classmates whereas others with comparable needs received far less.
The critical factor seemed to be teachers' awareness of individual
pupils' need for additional guidance and explanation. When
teachers were so aware, they were happy to spend further time
with individuals as necessary. Many pupils with special needs,
however, are adept at appearing to understand and keeping a
low profile. (An alternative tactic to mask a failure to understand
is of course to engage in disruptive behaviour.) This seemed to
be a regular feature of many classrooms observed in the course
of our study: hearing impaired pupils followed their peers
keenly, raising their hands when they did and going along with
activities without really understanding what they were doing;
visually impaired pupils went to great lengths to conceal their
difficulties, not acknowledging problems in reading from the
board or from poorly duplicated sheets; generally, pupils with
learning difficulties refrained from participating in class activities that might 'show them up'. Unfortunately, these low-
profile tactics seemed to work, particularly in large classes and
with teachers who were not versed in special needs, and many
pupils received less instructional time from teachers than they
needed.

Just as written handouts and workcards need to be adapted to
the learning needs of pupils, verbal interaction likewise should
be adjusted on the part of the teacher. Speech must obviously be
related to pupils' level of language development, and a balance
found between pupils' everyday language and any technical
terms or formal discourse judged necessary. The type of
questioning used is a further consideration. Many teachers
tended to use 'closed' questions (allowing for a single correct
answer only), which had the effect of discouraging pupils from
making all but the briefest of responses, when a more open-

ended approach would encourage pupil verbalization and enable the teacher to give more specific instruction.

Regular reinforcement is another feature of the teaching process which is no less important for pupils with special needs than for other pupils. Many indeed, particularly those with moderate learning difficulties, need extrinsic reinforcement in greater measure and for longer periods than their peers. Some teachers found this difficult, remarking on the seeming inability of pupils to work without constant reassurance that they were doing the right thing. This was not something they expected to have to provide particularly at secondary level and, while pupils must develop independent working habits, teachers needed to appreciate that some pupils had to be weaned away from dependence on constant reassurance in a very slow and gradual way.

Monitoring pupil progress should be an integral part of teaching as far as all pupils are concerned. It takes on particular import in the case of pupils with special educational needs, not only because they can present greater pedagogical demands but also their programmes of work are often individualized and cut across the school's mainstream arrangements. Schools' practice in this area was still evolving – with much space for progress in some cases – although the need for a systematic monitoring of progress was generally appreciated.

Records of various kinds were a major feature of the schools' practice. Some schools had designed special forms for recording work covered and progress made on a weekly or even daily basis. In more developed cases the recording format was implicit in the breakdown of the curriculum and grew out of it: a written statement of the tasks/activities pupils should engage in, the resource materials to be used and the criteria for successful task completion implied a clear and detailed assessment procedure. Staff meetings were another way of checking progress and while they could be unfocused they had the advantage of being interactive. Informal meetings between individual staff were common but a number of schools timetabled regular meetings for the purpose of discussing pupils' progress.

Class teachers' efforts can be supplemented by the judicious use of additional help in the classroom. Such help was in some cases the deciding factor in enabling an individual pupil to join a mainstream lesson. In the schools studied this help was provided, in different ways, by teachers, by ancillary staff and by other pupils.

A small number of schools made use of a second teacher to provide support in mainstream classes. This teacher was in all cases a specialist teacher of pupils with special needs. The aim was to allow the mainstream teacher to proceed at a normal pace while ensuring that the pupil with special needs participated fully in the lesson. In practice, the arrangements fell into one of three types, with the second teacher working exclusively with the pupil with special needs, working mainly with that pupil but available to help other pupils as well, or working with a small group of pupils which generally but not necessarily included the pupil with special needs. The mainstream teacher continued to be responsible for the lesson, deciding on subject matter, and remained in overall charge of the class.

As mentioned above, ancillary staff were given a specifically educational role in some schools. In the classroom this generally entailed working alongside a given pupil or having a watching brief on a pupil while carrying out general duties. It was policy in many schools that an ancillary would accompany a pupil with special needs joining a mainstream class for the first time. As the pupil became established in the class, the ancillary devoted less time to him/her and was more available to other pupils. Many teachers felt that ancillary staff could be used far more in classrooms, at both primary and secondary levels; their presence facilitated pupil participation in lessons and enabled pupils to receive a degree of individual attention not otherwise possible.

A further source of help for pupils with special needs came from fellow pupils. This was either offered spontaneously or organized by staff with pupils assigned to help on a rota basis. Sometimes the help was of a purely logistical kind, transporting equipment or fetching materials, but there was often a didactic element also, as when pupils assisted in experimental work or explained instructions that had been given to the whole class.

Bibliography

ALLSOP, J. (1980). 'Mainstreaming physically handicapped students', *Journal of Research and Development in Education*, 13, 4, 37–44.

ANDERSON, E.M. (1973). *The Disabled School Child*. London: Methuen Co.

BARRAGA, N.C. (1970). *Teachers Guide for Development of Visual Learning and Utilisation of Low Vision*. Louisville: American Printing House for the Blind.

BARRAGA, N.C. (1976). *Visual Handicaps and Learning*. Belmont, California: Wadsworth Publishing Co. Inc.

BAUM, B.R. and BRAZITA, R.F. (1979). 'Educating the exceptional child in the regular classroom', *Journal of Teacher Education*, 30, 6, 20–21.

BIGGE, J. and SIRVIS, B. (1978). 'Children with physical and multiple disabilities'. In: HARING, N.G. (Ed) *Behaviour of Exceptional Children*. Columbus, Ohio: Charles E. Merrill.

BLANK, H.R. (1958). 'Dreams of the Blind', *The Psychoanalytic Quarterly*, 27, 158–74.

BYFORD, E.M. (1979). 'Mainstreaming: the effect of regular teacher training programmes', *Journal of Teacher Education*, 30, 6, 23–4.

COPE, C. and ANDERSON, E. (1977). *Special Units in Ordinary Schools*. London: University of London Institute of Education.

CRATTY, B.J. (1971). *Movement and spatial awareness in blind children and youth*. Springfield, Ill.: Charles C. Thomas.

CRATTY, B.J. and SAMS, T.A. (1968). *The Body Image of Blind Children*. New York: American Foundation for the Blind.

CULTHANE, B. and CURWIN, R. (1978). 'There's a deaf child in my class', *Learning*, 7, 2, 111–13.

CUTSFORTH, T.D. (1951). *The Blind in School and Society: a psychological study*. New York: American Foundation for the Blind.

DAVIES, E. (1980). 'Primary School Records'. In: BURGESS, T. and ADAMS, E. (Eds) *Outcomes of Education*. London: Macmillan.

DUNN, L.M. (Ed) (1963). *Exceptional Children in the Schools: special education in transition*. New York: Holt, Rinehart and Winston, Inc.

FOSTER, J. (1971). *Recording Individual Progress.* London: Macmillan.
GEARHEART, B.R. and WEISHAHN, M.W. (1980). *The Handicapped Student in the Regular Classroom.* St. Louis: C.V. Mosby Co.
GONZALES, R. (1980). 'Mainstreaming your hearing impaired child in 1980: still an oversimplification', *Journal of Research and Development in Education,* 13, 4, 15–21.
GOUGH, E.R. (1981). 'Some psychological considerations in the education of blind students'. In: CORRICK, H.E. (Ed) *Teaching Handicapped Students Science: a resource handbook for 11–12 teachers.* Washington D.C.: National Education Association.
GREAT BRITAIN. DEPARTMENT OF EDUCATION AND SCIENCE (1972). *The Education of the Visually Handicapped.* London: HMSO.
GREAT BRITAIN. DEPARTMENT OF EDUCATION AND SCIENCE (1981). *Education Act 1981.* London: HMSO.
GREAT BRITAIN. DEPARTMENT OF EDUCATION AND SCIENCE (1983). Circular 1/83. *Assessments and Statements of Special Education Needs.* London: HMSO.
GREER, J.G. and ALLSOP, J. (1978). 'Adapting the learning environment for the hearing impaired, visually impaired and physically handicapped'. In: ANDERSON, R.M., GREER, J.G. and ODLE, S.J. (Eds) *Individualising materials for special children in mainstream.* Baltimore: University Park Press.
GRIFFING, B.L. (1970). 'Planning Education Programmes and Services for the Hard of Hearing. In: BERG, F. and FLETCHER, S.G. (Eds) *The Hard of Hearing Child: Clinical and Educational Management.* New York: Grune and Stratton.
HARLEY, R.K. JNR. (1963). 'Children with visual disabilities'. In: DUNN, L.M. (Ed) *Exceptional Children in the Schools.* New York: Holt, Rinehart and Winston, Inc.
HEDGCOCK, D. (1974). 'Facilitating integration at the junior high level', *Volta Review,* 76, 3, 182–8.
HEGARTY, S. (1982). 'Meeting special educational needs in the ordinary school', *Educational Research,* 24, 3, 174–81.
HEGARTY, S., POCKLINGTON, K. and LUCAS, D. (1982). *Integration in Action: case studies in the integration of pupils with special needs.* Windsor:NFER-NELSON.
HEGARTY, S. and POCKLINGTON, K. (1981). *Educating Pupils with Special Needs in the Ordinary School.* Windsor: NFER-NELSON.
HOBEN, M. (1980). 'Toward integration in the mainstream', *Exceptional Children,* 47, 2, 100–105.
JAMIESON, M., PARLETT, M. and POCKLINGTON, K. (1977). *Towards Integration: a study of blind and partially sighted children in ordinary schools.* Windsor: NFER.
JENSEMA, C.J. (1975). 'The relationship between academic achievement and the demographic characteristics of hearing impaired

children and youths'. In: *Series R, N.2*, Washington, D.C.: Office of Demographic Studies, Gallaudet College.

JENSEMA, C.J. and TRYBUS, R.J. (1978). 'Communication Patterns and Educational Achievement of Hearing Impaired Students'. In: *Series T, N.2*, Washington, D.C.: Office of Demographic Studies, Gallaudet College.

JOHNSON, D.W. and JOHNSON, R.T. (1980). 'Integrating students into the mainstream', *Exceptional Children*, 47, 2, 90–98.

KIERNAN, C.C. and KAVANAGH, S. (1977). Nightingale Integration Project. Final report to Scoial Science Research Council, London.

LAUDER, C. E., KANTHAR, H., MYERS, G. and RESNICK, J. (1978). 'Educational Placement of Children with Spina Bifida', *Exceptional Children*, 45, 432–7.

LOWENFIELD, B. (Ed) (1973). *The Visually Handicapped Child in School*. New York: John Day Co.

LYNAS, W. (1978). 'Integration and the Education of Hearing Impaired Children', *The Teacher of the Deaf*, 3, 1, 7–15.

LYNAS, W. (1981). 'Integration and Teaching Styles', *Special Education: Forward Trends*, 8, 3, 11–14.

MIDDLETON, E., MORSINK, C. and COHEN, D. (1979). 'Programme graduates' perception of need for training in main-streaming', *Exceptional Children*, 45, 4, 256–71.

NORTHCOTT, W.H. (1973). *The Hearing Impaired Child in a Regular Classroom: pre-school elementary and secondary years*. Washington: Alexander Graham Bell Association for the Deaf Inc.

PASANELLA, A.L. and VOLKMOR, C.B. (Eds) (1981). *Teaching Handicapped Students in Mainstream*. Colombus, Ohio: Charles E. Merrill.

POCKLINGTON, K. and HEGARTY, S. (1983). *The Development of a Language Unit: an evaluation of Rose Hill Language Unit, Oxford*. Slough: NFER.

REYNOLDS, M. and BIRCH, J. (1977). *Teaching Exceptional Children in All America's Schools: a first course for teachers and principals*. Relson, Va.: Council for Exceptional Children.

SCHLAEGEL, T.J. JNR. (1953). 'The dominant method of imagery in the blind as compared to sighted adolescents', *Journal of Genetic Psychology*, 83, 265–77.

SCHULTZ, L.R. (1982). 'Educating the Special Needs Student in the Regular Classroom', *Exceptional Children*, 48, 4, 366–8.

SHIPMAN, M. (1983). *Assessment in Primary and Middle School*. London: Croom HELM.

SIMON, E.P. and GILLMAN, A.E. (1979). 'Mainstreaming Visually Handicapped Pre-Schoolers, *Exceptional Children*, 6, 463–4.

SPENCER, M. (1980). 'Wheelchairs in a Primary School', *Special Education: Forward Trends*, 7, 1, 18–20.

STOKOE, W. (1976). 'The study and use of Sign Language', *Sign Language Studies*, 10, 1–36.

VERNON REPORT. GREAT BRITAIN. DEPARTMENT OF EDU-
CATION AND SCIENCE (1972). *The Education of the Visually
Handicapped.* London: HMSO.
VON HIPPEL, C. (1977). *Mainstreaming pre-schoolers: children with visual
handicaps.* Belmont, Mass.: Contract Research Corporation.
WARNOCK REPORT. GREAT BRITAIN. PARLIAMENT. HOUSE
OF COMMONS (1978). *Special Educational Needs.* Report of the
Committee of Inquiry into Education of Handicapped Children and
Young People. London: HMSO.
WOOD, F. and HIRSHOREN, A. (1981). 'The Hearing Impaired in the
Mainstream: the problem and some successful practices', *Journal for
Special Educators,* 17, 3, 291–302.

Index